AUSSIEDOODLE BIBLE
AND
AUSSIEDOODLES

Your Perfect Aussiedoodle Guide

AUSSIEDOODLES, AUSSIEDOODLE PUPPIES, AUSSIEDOODLE DOGS, AUSSIEDOODLE TRAINING, AUSSIEDOODLE SIZE, AUSSIEDOODLE NUTRITION, AUSSIEDOODLE HEALTH, BREEDERS, & MORE!

By Mark Manfield

I0089200

Published by DYM Worldwide Publishers 2019.

ISBN: 978-1-913154-12-7

Copyright © DYM Worldwide Publishers, 2019
2 Lansdowne Row, Number 240 London W1J 6HL

will not be liable for, the websites being temporarily or being removed from the Internet. The accuracy and completeness of the information provided herein, and opinions stated herein are not guaranteed or warranted to produce any particular results, and the advice or strategies, contained herein may not be suitable for every individual. The author, publisher, distributors, and/or affiliates shall not be liable for any loss incurred as a consequence of the use and application, directly or indirectly of any information presented in this work. This publication is designed to provide information regarding the subject matter covered. The information included in this book has been compiled to give an overview of the topics covered. The information contained in this book has been compiled to provide an overview of the subject. It is not intended as medical advice and should not be construed as such. For a firm diagnosis of any medical conditions, you should consult a doctor or veterinarian (as related to animal health). The writer, publisher, distributors, and/or affiliates of this work are not responsible for any damages or negative consequences following any of the treatments or methods highlighted in this book.

Website links are for informational purposes only and should not be seen as a personal endorsement; the same applies to any products or services mentioned in this work. The reader should also be aware that although the web links included were correct at the time of this writing, they may become out of date in the future. Any pricing or currency exchange rate information was accurate at the time of writing but may become out of date in the future. The Author, Publisher, distributors, and/or affiliates assume no responsibility for pricing and currency exchange rates mentioned within this work.

Table of Contents

Introduction xi

Chapter 1 – Aussiedoodle History and Origins 15

What is an Aussiedoodle? 16

Where Did the Aussiedoodle Come From? 19

What Was the Original Purpose of
the Aussiedoodle? 20

Is the Aussiedoodle an Old Breed? 20

How is the Aussiedoodle Different from the
Labradoodle or Goldendoodle? 20

Chapter 2 – Aussiedoodle Dogs—What Do You
Need to Know? 23

Are You Prepared to Handle the Needs of
an Aussiedoodle? 24

Do Aussiedoodles Make Good Family Pets? 25

Common Aussiedoodle Coat Types 26

Common Aussiedoodle Coat Colors 28

What is the Aussiedoodle's Temperament Like? 31

What Behavior Can You Expect from Your
Aussiedoodle? 33

How Long Do Aussiedoodles Live? 34

What Jobs Can the Aussiedoodle Dog Do? 34

Can an Aussiedoodle Be a Show Dog? 35

Are Aussiedoodles Good Hunters? 35

Do Aussiedoodles Get Along with
Other Animals?..36
Are Aussiedoodles Good with Children?...................36
Popular Names for Aussiedoodle Puppies 37

Chapter 3 – Aussiedoodle Types..39
Miniature Aussiedoodles 39
Standard Aussiedoodles...40
Teacup Aussiedoodles 40
Are Aussiedoodles a Recognized Breed?...................40

Chapter 4 – Aussiedoodle Breeders and Buying an Aussiedoodle
—How to Find a Quality Aussiedoodle.....................41
Aussiedoodle Puppies for Sale—What Should
You Look for? 43
Important Questions to Ask Aussiedoodle Breeders ...48
What Can You Expect to Pay for an Aussiedoodle?...52
Buying an Adult Aussiedoodle—What Must
You Consider?..52

Chapter 5 – Aussiedoodle Adoption—Adopting an
Aussiedoodle Puppy or Adult Dog...........................55
Understanding a Rescue Aussiedoodle's Past.............56
Rescued Aussiedoodles—Special Care 56
Reputable Aussiedoodle Rescues 57
Finding Aussiedoodles for Adoption Near Me 58
Giving Back—Volunteering with an
Aussiedoodle Rescue 59

Chapter 6 – Aussiedoodle Supplies—What Do You Need?..........61
Aussiedoodle Food—What is the Best Food
and Where Do You Find It? 62
Aussiedoodle Beds—What is the Most Comfortable
Bedding for Your Aussiedoodle?..............................66

Aussiedoodle Collars—How Do You Get the Right Fit? 71

Aussiedoodle Leashes—How Do You Choose a Style and Length? 72

Aussiedoodle Harnesses—Is a Harness a Good Choice for an Aussiedoodle? 73

Aussiedoodle Kennels—How Do You Select the Right Size? 74

Aussiedoodle Dog Houses—How Do You Choose a Size and What Features Do You Need?......75

Aussiedoodle Toys—What Selection Should You Make to Keep Your Dog Stimulated? 76

Aussiedoodle Dog Treats—How Do You Choose Safe and Yummy Snacks for Your Aussiedoodle? 77

Aussiedoodle Muzzles—How Do You Make Sure the Muzzle Fits? 81

Chapter 7 – Aussiedoodle Needs—How Can You Best Take Care Of Your Aussiedoodle? 85

Basic Care of the Aussiedoodle 85

Aussiedoodle Puppies—What Do You Need to Know?......86

How Much Exercise Should Your Aussiedoodle Puppy Get? 87

Chapter 8 – Aussiedoodle Grooming—How Can You Make It Fun and Easy?......89

Aussiedoodle Grooming Basics 90

Aussiedoodle Dog Shampoos— Recommended Types 94

Aussiedoodle Brushes—The Best Types for an Aussiedoodle's Coat 95

Cleaning a Dirty Aussiedoodle 96

Do Aussiedoodles Shed?......97

Are Aussiedoodles Hypoallergenic? 97

Finding a Professional Groomer for
Your Aussiedoodle 98

Chapter 9 –   Aussiedoodle Training—Successfully
Training Your Aussiedoodle.....................................99

What Tools Do You Need for
Aussiedoodle Training? 100

What Treats Are Good for Positive Reinforcement
Training for Your Aussiedoodle? 100

What Does Your Aussiedoodle Need to Learn? 102

How Do You Deal with Unwanted
Aussiedoodle Behaviors? 105

How Do You Properly Socialize
Your Aussiedoodle?..107

Can You Train Your Aussiedoodle to Swim? 109

Is It a Good Idea to Train Your Aussiedoodle
with a Shock Collar? 110

Chapter 10 – Aussiedoodle Breeding—Getting Your
Aussiedoodle Ready for a Litter 111

Necessary Health Testing for Prospective
Aussiedoodle Breeding Dogs 114

The Female Aussiedoodle—Getting Ready
for Breeding 118

The Male Aussiedoodle—Getting Ready
for Breeding 119

Sourcing a Good Quality Aussiedoodle Stud Dog ...120

Newborn Aussiedoodle Puppies—Their Care
and Feeding 121

Chapter 11 – Aussiedoodle Lifestyle—What is it Like to Live
with an Aussiedoodle? 123

Becoming a Savvy Aussiedoodle Owner 124

Getting Your House Ready for Your Aussie
doodle Puppy 125

Are Cages a Good Idea for an Aussiedoodle?...........126

Do You Need a Kennel for an Aussiedoodle? 127

Aussiedoodles and Dog Doors—Do You Need
a Dog Door in Your Home?.....................................127

Aussiedoodles and Dog Gates—Do You Need
to Install a Dog Gate?...128

Should You Allow Your Aussiedoodle on
Your Furniture? 128

Chapter 12 – Aussiedoodle Health—What Do You
Need to Know?..129

What are Common Aussiedoodle
Health Problems?..129

Aussiedoodles and Bloat—Is Bloat a Problem
for the Aussiedoodle?..131

What Vaccinations Will Your Aussiedoodle Need? 132

Should You Give Your Aussiedoodle Vitamins?......133

Keeping Your Aussiedoodle at a Healthy Weight....133

What is a Healthy Amount of Food for an
Aussiedoodle? 134

Chapter 13 – Aussiedoodles—The Golden Years 137

Aussiedoodle Changes in the Golden Years 137

Aussiedoodle Health—Caring for Your
Geriatric Aussiedoodle 138

Aussiedoodle Endings—Saying Goodbye to
Your Senior Aussiedoodle 140

Chapter 14 – Conclusion..143

BONUS CHAPTER Your Comprehensive Aussiedoodle
Resource List 147

Introduction

Highly intelligent and with energy to spare, the Aussiedoodle is one of the newest dog breeds to hit the scene. A combination of two purebred breeds known for their trainability and keen sense of "smarts," the Aussiedoodle is a bundle of fun in one adorable, compact canine package. Known as a "hybrid" or "designer dog breed," the Aussiedoodle is typical of medium build and comes in a variety of coat colors and textures. A breed that is exceptionally affectionate, the Aussiedoodle is a true family dog, making it an ideal choice for families with children. Aussiedoodles are characterized by their high energy levels, and they thrive when given a job to do. With such an intense drive to please coupled with their highly intelligent nature, the Aussiedoodle is the perfect companion for hiking, running, agility, and other performance sports. A crossbreed, the Aussiedoodle is not yet recognized by any kennel club. Their purpose is entirely to be a companion dog, a job at which they excel. Believed to be hypoallergenic but unsupported by any scientific evidence, some Aussiedoodles are born with coats that resemble the Poodle portion of their pedigree, making them low shedding as a general rule. For those that favor the Australian Shepherd side of their pedigree, they do shed more frequently than those that take after the Poodle. Exuberant and friendly by nature, the Aussiedoodle has a sweet, happy temperament.

Aussiedoodles are a true family dog
and are excellent companions for children.

The International Designer Canine Registry, a governing body which offers registration services and pedigree tracking for mixed breeds, crossbreeds, and hybrids, describes the Aussiedoodle as "…very intelligent, loyal, active, and affectionate. The Aussiedoodle is generally an agile, playful, and sharp dog."

The Aussiedoodle, sometimes affectionately referred to as an "Aussiepoo," is not yet consistent in appearance as a relatively new breed that is a cross between the purebred Standard, Miniature, or Toy Poodle and the Standard or Miniature Australian Shepherd. This diversity in appearance and personality traits is endearing to those who know and love the breed. At present, the Aussiedoodle has no definitive history, though the breed was believed to have been derived out of a desire to produce a true canine "Einstein," possessing the intelligence, stamina, and drive to excel at work and play. As with most dog breeds, it is important to socialize the Aussiedoodle early and often to ensure the dog is exposed to many new and different stimuli. Though easy to train, the Aussiedoodle can struggle with focus. On the whole, this breed thrives under positive reinforcement training, which will be further explained in Chapter 9. If not exercised daily or given a job to do, the Aussiedoodle can become neurotic, obsessive, and even destructive.

The Aussiedoodle enjoys an excellent life expectancy, which typically ranges from 10-13 years of age. A breed which is known to enjoy good health, hip dysplasia is the one major health concern in Aussiedoodles. Other less frequently seen diseases or conditions include Von Willebrand's Disease, Cataracts, and Bloat.

Aussiedoodles do not thrive when kept indoors for extended periods. An active breed, the Aussiedoodle is most content with regular mental and physical stimulation. Puzzle games that require the Aussiedoodle to challenge its brain are the perfect means to keep this breed occupied.

A highly enthusiastic greeter, you will never feel lonely with an Aussiedoodle around! A true "people dog," the Aussiedoodle needs to be with its people as much as possible and will become depressed if forced to be isolated for any length of time. Care must be taken to teach the Aussiedoodle manners, particularly if the dog shares its home with children as its boundless energy and penchant for knocking things over can be overwhelming for little ones. The Aussiedoodle is both fun-loving and adorable. To meet one is to love one, and many families do!

CHAPTER 1

Aussiedoodle History and Origins

A relatively new dog breed, there is no clearly defined history for the Aussiedoodle, beyond its genetic descendants. It is believed that the breed originated in Australia, though today, the Aussiedoodle's popularity is largely found in the United States. The Aussiedoodle is a highly prized family companion dog. Known for their happy, friendly nature, they are perfectly suited to the active, busy lifestyle of a family with kids, and their resilience allows them to adapt well to new environments and routines. History is now being written for this beloved crossbreed.

The Aussiedoodle is a crossbreed which takes half of its pedigree from the Poodle, whether Standard (pictured above), Miniature, or Toy.

The name Aussiedoodle is derived from the two purebred dogs which were combined to create this new designer dog breed. Selectively bred for specific traits, the Aussiedoodle was borne out of a desire to create a dog of great intelligence and high trainability.

What is an Aussiedoodle?

The Aussiedoodle is what is known as a crossbreed. Crossbreeds are created by combining two dogs of purebred heritage to create a new breed which is ideally a mixture of the best traits of both dogs. In the case of the Aussiedoodle, either a Standard or Miniature Australian Shepherd is bred to a Standard, Miniature, or Toy Poodle to create this exciting hybrid. To reflect the combination of these two beloved, noble breeds, the names were combined into an affectionate handle: the Aussiedoodle.

The Aussiedoodle is also commonly referred to as an Aussiepoo though some serious breeders reject this name. As a relatively new breed, there is no set date to reference for the development of the Aussiedoodle. It is a rather new phenomenon, but the breed is so well-beloved, that the Aussiedoodle is sure to become a permanent fixture in the homes of dog lovers around the world.

Though the Aussiedoodle itself cannot boast of having a long breed history, both the Australian Shepherd and the Poodle have a detailed and rich heritage they bring to the breed. As a herding breed, the Australian Shepherd is a dog known for its boundless energy and loyalty. It is from the Australian Shepherd that the Aussiedoodle inherits its ability to bond deeply with people. The Australian Shepherd has often been referred to as a canine "Einstein," a trait it shares in common with the Poodle. An exceptionally high energy breed intended to be a working dog, the Australian Shepherd is full of work ethic and stamina and requires a job to do to remain content. Highly intelligent and driven to please, the Australian Shepherd lives for its "people." Legend dictates that this breed originated in the Pyrenees Mountains of France and Spain in what is known as "Basque" country. During the 1800s, many Basque shepherds and their dogs made the trek to Australia to pursue more fertile ranchlands for cattle farming. This early type of Australian Shepherd was known as the "Pyrenean Shepherd." Once settled in Australia, these Basque shepherds selectively bred their Pyrenean Shepherds to Collies and Border Collies in an attempt to produce the ideal herding dog. Visiting California ranchers admired the strong work ethic of this new crossbreed and mistook them for a breed of Australian heritage when labeling them the "Australian Shepherd," the name this breed takes today. Today, the breed has been further developed in the United States into the fine herding dog and family companion we know and love.

By comparison, the Standard Poodle, a dog claimed as the national dog of France originated as a duck hunting breed in Germany. It is from the Poodle that the Aussiedoodle takes its water-loving ways. A breed that is over 400 years old, the Poodle's coat is considered to be low to no-shedding, a desirable trait that Aussiedoodle breeders strive to produce in their cross-bred puppies. A dog with excellent retrieving skills, the Poodle is a breed whose intelligence surpasses even that of the savvy Australian Shepherd. Due to their elegant looks and regal posture, the Poodle soon moved from the duck hunter's side into the homes of the elite where it remains a pampered pooch today. The Poodle also possesses an incredibly acute sense of scent, making them suited to work as truffle hunters.

It is not difficult to see how combining these two breeds could create a powerhouse canine capable of fierce intelligence, incredibly deep bonds with their families, and the looks and personality to make the perfect canine companion. This is the dog that we know as the Aussiedoodle.

The Australian Shepherd (pictured above) is the other purebred breed which makes up the Aussiedoodle's pedigree.

Where Did the Aussiedoodle Come From?

Though the Aussiedoodle's origins are largely unknown, Australia receives the credit for the original pairing of these two breeds. It is possible that after the highly successful pairing of the Golden Retriever and Poodle to create the Goldendoodle and the Labrador Retriever and the Poodle to create the Labradoodle that other like-minded breeders desiring a dog of deep intelligence and low-shedding properties decided to mate an Australian Shepherd to a Poodle. Obviously, this breeding cross was considered a victory as the breed endures today, having gained much popularity in the United States in particular.

What Was the Original Purpose of the Aussiedoodle?

The Aussiedoodle found its original purpose as a companion dog of high intelligence and loyalty. Intended to be easily trainable, the Aussiedoodle is ideally suited to work as a therapy dog. The Aussiedoodle is also in possession of intense drive, making it the perfect teammate for sports such as flyball, disc dog, and agility. The primary purpose of the Aussiedoodle is to make life more enjoyable for its family, a role it excels in.

Is the Aussiedoodle an Old Breed?

The precise age of the breed is not known as its origins are relatively new. We do know that the Aussiedoodle is not an old breed. It has gained such a popular following that it is sure to retain its position in family homes as well as in the dog sports performance arena.

How is the Aussiedoodle Different from the Labradoodle or Goldendoodle?

The primary difference between these three breeds lies in their parentage. An Aussiedoodle is produced from a mating between a purebred Australian Shepherd, whether Standard or Miniature, and a purebred Poodle, also Standard, Miniature, or Toy.
The Goldendoodle came into existence through combining a purebred Golden Retriever with a Standard or Miniature Poodle with a Labradoodle being a pairing between a purebred Labrador Retriever and a purebred Standard or Miniature Poodle. Since the Goldendoodle and the Labradoodle enjoy a longer breed history than that of the Aussiedoodle, they are now sufficient generations away from the original breeding that the gene pool

is wide enough to allow for a Goldendoodle to be bred to a Goldendoodle and a Labradoodle to a Labradoodle. So, this means it is not advised to breed an Aussiedoodle direct to an Aussiedoodle, to avoid potential health complications that could arise. At this time, the Aussiedoodle is too close to its inception to have enough genetic diversity to follow in the footsteps of its Poodle hybrid predecessors. This will come in time.

CHAPTER 2

Aussiedoodle Dogs—
What Do You Need to Know?

This chapter is dedicated to learning more about the Aussiedoodle's appearance and characteristics. Unlike purebred breeds, there is no definitive "standard," which outlines how an Aussiedoodle should look or act. Why is this? While purebred dogs have enjoyed many generations to refine their particular look into a consistent set of traits, the Aussiedoodle is a relatively new breed and is a composite of two purebred breeds that are available in different sizes. This means that even the Aussiedoodle's size and weight will not be consistent. Since genetics are a random game at best, the combination of an Australian Shepherd and a Poodle could produce a lot of different traits in the two dogs' offspring. It is possible that the puppies from this type of breeding may favor the physical appearance of one parent over another, meaning your Aussiedoodle puppy may more closely resemble an Australian Shepherd or a Poodle, instead of being the ideal blend of the two breeds. Also equally possible is that the resulting puppies may possess all of the best traits of the two parent dogs...or all of the worst. This is also true of breeding two purebred dogs of the same breed together; however, decades and sometimes even centuries of highly selective breeding ensure that purebred breeds will retain the same basic appearance and personality traits.

Is the Aussiedoodle the dog for you? This chapter will help you better understand what life is like with an Aussiedoodle, and if your family is up to the challenge.

Are You Prepared to Handle the Needs of an Aussiedoodle?

The average Aussiedoodle is really no more work than any other dog, with the exception of the need to satisfy an exceptionally high drive with exercise. The biggest question you will need to ask yourself is this: Are you prepared to take your dog for frequent walks or runs each day? Aussiedoodles will not do well in a home where they live the life of a pampered couch potato. In fact, it is quite the opposite. The Aussiedoodle is a very happy breed, but this sense of fulfillment only occurs when the dog's needs are properly met. The Aussiedoodle requires consistent daily mental and physical activity to thrive. This is considered a standard part of care for the breed. If this is not something you are able to offer, it is best to consider another breed of dog that is better suited to your lifestyle.

Another factor for you to keep in mind is the fact that the Aussiedoodle is not a low maintenance breed when it comes to grooming. Since the Aussiedoodle's coat can more closely resemble the Australian Shepherd portion of its pedigree, you will need to brush your dog's coat daily to keep it from becoming matted. Unfortunately, Aussiedoodle coats are also known to trap odors, making them require more frequent bathing to remain smelling fresh and clean. This will require the purchase of a blow dryer as you will need to thoroughly dry your dog's coat then comb it once dry to keep it from tangling. While a groomer can greatly assist your efforts to keep your Aussiedoodle looking and smelling good, you will still be required to provide grooming maintenance every day in order to keep your dog's coat from knotting and matting, something that is incredibly painful for your dog. You could opt to completely shave your dog down every few months; however, daily brushing is still recommended. However, to maintain a shaved coat, your Aussiedoodle will still need to see a professional groomer every six to eight weeks. You will need to understand that this grooming will take up a lot of your time and will also cost you a lot of money.

Do Aussiedoodles Make Good Family Pets?

Aussiedoodles are known to be exceptional family pets. Extremely friendly, happy by nature, and deeply affectionate, the Aussiedoodle loves children. It is important to note that the Aussiedoodle is a playful breed and has moderate to high activity needs. Their exuberant nature can be overwhelming to very young children and to the elderly, but they mean no harm; they are simply dogs who really love life. Aussiedoodles are highly enthusiastic, and this natural excitability can cause them to accidentally knock things over, including household items and small children! For this reason, it is important to begin "manners" training with an Aussiedoodle right away to help the dog learn to cope with its natural exuberance in an appropriate fashion. If adding an Aussiedoodle to your home is part of your plans, you will need to be certain you are willing to make the necessary commitment to exercising your dog daily. In addition to this, you will need to provide a fenced yard to keep your Aussiedoodle safe and to offer it the opportunity to stretch its legs throughout the day. Though only a dog of medium build, it is essential that a prospective Aussiedoodle owner be financially prepared to meet the needs of this charming breed.

The Aussiedoodle is the dog for you if you are looking for one that …

- Is medium in size.
- Has higher grooming requirements than average.
- Is friendly and affectionate.
- Is known for exuberance and easy excitability.
- Requires frequent and regular exercise.
- Benefits from having a "job" to do.

The Aussiedoodle may not be the best choice for you if…

- You expect your house to remain pristine.
- You do not want to commit to an active lifestyle.
- You are not interested in proper obedience training to ensure your dog is mannerly.
- You are not prepared to brush your dog regularly to prevent matting or to make frequent trips to the groomer to properly maintain your Aussiedoodle's coat.

Common Aussiedoodle Coat Types

It is believed that part of the original intent in breeding an Australian Shepherd to a Poodle was to produce a dog that was low to no-shedding, and typically, this is the type of coat you will get in an Aussiedoodle puppy. The average Aussiedoodle's coat is known to be velvety soft and fluffy. Since the coat is less prone to shed, many feel the Aussiedoodle is an ideal companion for families who suffer from allergies. As the Aussiedoodle is a crossbreed, it is possible that an Aussiedoodle puppy may retain more genes from the Australian Shepherd portion of its pedigree. If this is the case, the puppy would be more likely to exhibit a coat that is straighter and longer than the tighter, curlier coat of the Poodle. Most commonly, breeders are able to identify what type of coat each Aussiedoodle puppy will have when the puppies have reached five to six weeks of age. It is important to note that even within a single litter coat type can vary from puppy to puppy.

Aussiedoodles come in many different colors and coat types.

Common Aussiedoodle Coat Colors

Since Aussiedoodles are a hybrid, their coat colors can vary dramatically depending on the lineage behind the Australian Shepherd and Poodle selected for each individual breed pairing.

The Four "Accepted" Colors for Australian Shepherds

As an AKC registered breed, there are four acceptable colors defined in the Australian Shepherd's breed standard. Other colors may occur but would be unusual and would then be considered a disqualification for any owners with hopes of showing their dog. The four accepted colors for Australian Shepherds are:

- Black
- Blue Merle—Blue merle is typified by a mixture of black, grey, and silver tones which give the appearance of a "blue" coat.
- Red
- Red Merle—Red merle is a mixture of red, silver, and what is known as "buff."

White and "copper" patches are also acceptable on the coat of an Australian Shepherd. For many owners, tri-colored Australian Shepherds are the most desirable of all.

The "Accepted" Colors for Poodles

The AKC recognizes a large number of colors for Standard, Miniature, and Toy Poodles. In addition to accepted colors and color combinations, there are also preferred color markings. Here is a list of the colors and color markings accepted for Poodles by the American Kennel Club:

- Apricot
- Black
- Blue
- Brown
- Café au Lait (a shade of brown which poses slight fading properties)
- Cream
- Grey
- Red
- Silver
- Silver Beige
- White
- Black and Apricot
- Black and Brown
- Black and Cream
- Black and Grey
- Black and Red
- Black and Silver
- Black and Tan
- Black and White
- Blue and White
- Brown and Apricot
- Brown and White

- Cream and White
- Grey and White
- Red and Apricot
- Red and White
- White and Apricot
- White and Silver

Acceptable markings include:

- Black mask
- Black markings
- White markings
- White mask

Parti-colored Poodles, or Poodles with a coat that is white at its base with patches of any other color, are disqualified from showing.

So, what color can an Aussiedoodle be? The genetics of the specific Australian Shepherd and Poodle mating will determine the color of the puppies. Color genetics can be somewhat complicated to understand as certain colors are considered to be dominant over others, meaning they are sometimes predestined to reproduce themselves in offspring. In addition to this, both parents in the breeding pair will carry the genes of their ancestors, which means their offspring can produce colors and coat types that they themselves do not display. But it easy to see simply from looking at the list of possible colors for each of these breeds, that a wide variety of color combinations is possible in an Aussiedoodle puppy.

Aussiedoodles may come in solid colors, base colors with different colored markings, and some even develop tri-colored coats as they mature.

The Aussiedoodle Puppy Coat

Unlike other breeds, the Aussiedoodle will have some adult coat by the time the puppy reaches the age of five or six months. The puppy's coat will continue to change in color as the puppy matures; however, the texture typically remains the same. It is quite common for Aussiedoodle puppies who were born with very dark coats to lighten considerably as they age.

Most commonly, the Aussiedoodle puppy's coat will retain the soft, curly texture of the Poodle or the smooth, longer coat of the Australian Shepherd, but a happy medium of both coat types and textures is also possible.

The Aussiedoodle Adult Coat

By age nine months, the adult coat is well in place. Though it will take another nine to ten months for the process to be complete, the Aussiedoodle's true color and texture will be established by this point in time.

What is the Aussiedoodle's Temperament Like?

As the offspring of an Australian Shepherd and a Poodle, two breeds who share many traits in common, there are certain defined personality traits you will see in any Aussiedoodle. Aussiedoodles are fun-loving dogs with energy to spare. If you're the kind of person who is up for an adventure, your Aussiedoodle will be only too happy to come along!

A friendly and affectionate breed, Aussiedoodles never meet a stranger; everyone they come in contact with becomes a cherished friend. As lovers of children, they delight in play and are known to be gentle and tolerant in nature. Nicknamed the "Velcro dog," Aussiedoodles bond very quickly and deeply to their family members and thrive when by their side. Aussiedoodles are not dogs that do well when isolated from family life due to their penchant for highly sociable behavior.

The Aussiedoodle is incredibly smart, there is no disputing the intelligence of the breed. Highly trainable, the Aussiedoodle thrives learning new tricks and commands and excels at performance sports such as agility, flyball, Rally-O, and even competitive obedience.

Given that the background of both the Australian Shepherd and the Poodle lean towards hunting, retrieving, and herding, it is possible that your Aussiedoodle may have an incredibly high prey drive. With this in mind, it is important to provide a secure containment system for your Aussiedoodle. As dogs who exhibit prey drive, and who are born with the desire to work, Aussiedoodles can often be flight risks. A breed possessing intense intelligence, the Aussiedoodle can easily outsmart any fencing system, so it will be necessary to stay one step ahead of your dog to keep it safe.

Aussiedoodles can be prone to being overly sensitive. Care must be taken not to crush their spirit during training. This breed can also be quite stubborn and is often seemingly tireless. In order to avoid nuisance behaviors, vigorous daily exercise is not an option; it is a necessity. Failure to ensure the Aussiedoodle receives the physical and mental stimulation it requires can lead to annoying behaviors such as nuisance barking, digging, and general destruction.

What Behavior Can You Expect from Your Aussiedoodle?

If your Aussiedoodle receives regular daily exercise and mental stimulation, you will most likely have a very energetic, happy-go-lucky dog! Your Aussiedoodle will want to be by your side as often as you will allow it, so it is always a great idea to bring your dog along on any outings you undertake. This is part of the key to keeping your Aussiedoodle contented.

The Aussiedoodle truly is a joy-filled dog, and if kept productively engaged, nuisance behaviors are unlikely to develop. However, as a dog prone to overexcitability, it cannot be overemphasized how important it is to teach your Aussiedoodle manners and boundaries. It is not uncommon for Aussiedoodles to jump up. You will need to teach your Aussiedoodle to remain on the ground unless invited up on people's laps or furniture. While the Aussiedoodle's nature does not tend towards the polite inherently, there is never any malice in its intention. Your dog simply needs to learn its place in the order of your household.

As a dog with natural herding and hunting instincts, it is likely that your Aussiedoodle will want to chase small animals such as cats, rats, rabbits, rodents, and even smaller dogs. While prey drive is instinctual and cannot be trained out of a dog, you can ensure your dog's safety as well as the safety of other animals, by providing a fenced containment system your dog cannot escape. However, bear in mind that Aussiedoodles are master escape artists! In selecting the correct fencing for your yard, you will want to consider what methods of escape your dog prefers. Some Aussiedoodles will prefer climbing while others are happy to try to jump a fence or dig under it. Your dog's personal escape style will help you to select the best type of fencing for your Aussiedoodle.

But the most common behavior you can expect from your Aussiedoodle is lots and lots of affection. A loyal breed who longs to be by your side, you can expect lots of kisses and constant attention from your Aussiedoodle. If you value your alone time, you might want to consider another breed, because you won't be getting any of it when an Aussiedoodle joins your home!

How Long Do Aussiedoodles Live?

The average life expectancy of an Aussiedoodle is between 10 to 13 years. Though both the Poodle and the Australian Shepherd enjoy life expectancies of up to 15 years, the Aussiedoodle, to date, has not experienced such longevity. Though the breed is not predisposed to any particularly debilitating health conditions that might shorten its life span, it has been reported by owners of the breed that most commonly do not survive past 13 years of age, at a maximum. Still, this projected life expectancy offers a longer life which can be filled to the brim, with high-quality living. Of course, your Aussiedoodle's lifespan will be affected by the genetics of its parents, as well as its environment, and as such, results will vary from dog to dog and cannot be predicted.

What Jobs Can the Aussiedoodle Dog Do?

Aussiedoodles carry strong herding and hunting instincts and are a breed that thrives when given a job to do. Natural hunters, this breed excels out in the field hunting, retrieving ducks from the water, or even sniffing out truffles in the woods. The Poodle portion of the Aussiedoodle's heritage was cherished for its truffle hunting abilities and is still used for this purpose today. As a nod to the Australian Shepherd genes at play in the Aussiedoodle, this breed can potentially serve as a herding breed. If you happen to notice your Aussiedoodle circling your children to gather them into one central location, your dog has the herding instinct, for sure!

It has been said that Aussiedoodles can also fulfill the role of watchdog. However, though this breed will surely alert bark at the presence of a stranger; by nature, the Aussiedoodle is far too amiable to ever truly keep danger at bay. Also, like a dog that craves the companionship of its family, the Aussiedoodle is unlikely to thrive when left outside or alone in the family home on guard duty.

Can an Aussiedoodle Be a Show Dog?

Since the Aussiedoodle is a crossbreed, it is not a breed that is recognized by any official kennel club, at this time. For this reason, the Aussiedoodle cannot be shown in conformation events recognized by these clubs. However, since crossbreeds are permitted to compete in performance sports by such reputable kennel clubs as the AKC, they are more than welcome to enter such events as Rally-O, agility, or competitive obedience. At this time, there are no conformation events available for Aussiedoodles with the main designer dog registries known as the International Designer Canine Registry

Are Aussiedoodles Good Hunters?

Aussiedoodles are excellent hunting companions. A breed that thrives on teamwork and a close relationship with its owner, your

Aussiedoodle will happily accompany you into the brush, bush, or even the lake! Owing to its Poodle heritage, the Aussiedoodle is a natural in the water and excels at retrieving. Due to their natural prey drive, Aussiedoodles are prone to chase, which could assist their owners in driving quarry on a hunt.

Aussiedoodles also possess an excellent sense of smell, making them superior tracking dogs and well-suited to sourcing truffles alongside their owners.

Do Aussiedoodles Get Along with Other Animals?

Given to a genial nature, Aussiedoodles love other dogs! However, their natural exuberance can be off-putting to other breeds who may interpret their over the top behavior as threatening. To ensure your Aussiedoodle is dog-friendly, it is important to socialize the dog at a young age with other socially appropriate, well-mannered dogs.

Aussiedoodles can live peaceably with cats, but proper introductions should ensue at a young age to be certain of peaceful family relationships. If introducing an adult Aussiedoodle to your cat, you may find its natural tendency is to chase the cat, creating conflict between your two pets.

Are Aussiedoodles Good with Children?

Aussiedoodles are ideally suited to family life, and they adore children. They are a patient breed with gentle ways. However, the Aussiedoodle often is not aware of its size or strength, which is why obedience training from a young age is so necessary. It's important to teach your Aussiedoodle not to jump up on children, as their eagerness to greet could lead to an accident or injury.

As with all breeds, it is vital that all interactions between your Aussiedoodle and children be properly supervised. Even the most patient dog can become irritated by rough handling. To be certain of no unfortunate accidents and to protect both your Aussiedoodle and your child, you will want to be present to supervise all play time involving dogs and kids.

Popular Names for Aussiedoodle Puppies

Choosing an appropriate name for your Aussiedoodle is so much fun! In most families, everyone wants to get involved, and it can be quite a challenge to find just the right "handle" for your new Aussiedoodle friend.

Here is a list of some of the most common names for Aussiedoodle boys:

- Max
- Charlie
- Jack
- Toby
- Rocky
- Bear
- Zeus
- Thor
- Milo
- Blue
- Gunner
- Jax

Here is a list of popular names for Aussiedoodle girls:

- Bella
- Bentley
- Lucy
- Sophie
- Sadie
- Chloe
- Maggie
- Lola
- Coco
- Rosie
- Luna
- Nala

CHAPTER 3

Aussiedoodle Types

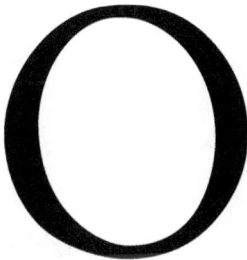

One of the great things about an Aussiedoodle is that they come in different sizes! Think a Standard is just a little too big for you? Why not get a Miniature instead?

Miniature Aussiedoodles

If you combine a Miniature Australian Shepherd with a Miniature Poodle, you will get a Miniature Aussiedoodle! A Miniature Aussiedoodle is the same great dog just in a smaller package. If you opt to add a Mini Aussiedoodle to your home, your dog will likely only reach 10-15 inches (25 -38 cm) in height and 15-35 lbs (7-16 kg) in weight. Some breeders may opt to breed a Toy Poodle to a Miniature Australian Shepherd which ideally would produce puppies that tend towards the smaller size. On the whole, the Miniature Aussiedoodle is considered a small to medium-sized dog. However, since this breed is an amalgamation of two purebred breeds, you never know what you will get! That's what makes Aussiedoodles so much fun.

Standard Aussiedoodles

In like fashion, breeding a Standard Australian Shepherd to a Standard Poodle will result in a Standard Aussiedoodle. Considerably larger than the miniature version, it is this variant that most lovers of the breed are most familiar with. Standard Aussiedoodles reach approximately 12-18 inches (30-46 cm) in height and can weigh in at up to 70 lbs (32 kg). Much like the Miniature Aussiedoodle, it is not known what to expect from breeding a Standard Australian Shepherd to a Standard Poodle since the breed is so new in its inception, and there is no definitive breed standard or history.

Teacup Aussiedoodles

Since neither the Australian Shepherd nor the Poodle is available in Teacup sizes, you should run from anyone advertising a Teacup Aussiedoodle. The Aussiedoodle is not a toy breed and cannot be produced in this size variant.

Are Aussiedoodles a Recognized Breed?

At this time, the Aussiedoodle remains an unrecognized breed. However, since most recognized purebreds today found their origins through selective breeding of several purebred breeds together to create a new hybrid, official recognition by a kennel club may come in time. Aussiedoodles are eligible for registration with several different agencies which recognize crossbreeds and track their pedigrees to provide a recorded history for the future.

CHAPTER 4

Aussiedoodle Breeders and Buying an Aussiedoodle— How to Find a Quality Aussiedoodle

Sourcing your Aussiedoodle puppy from a reputable breeder is the beginning of your journey. With the internet making it easy to find any breed of dog available anywhere in the world at any time, finding an Aussiedoodle puppy will not prove a challenge. However, you don't want to purchase just ANY Aussiedoodle puppy; you want one that is most likely to be healthy and displays a sound temperament. Since the breeding of hybrids is not regulated by any governing agency, anyone who owns an Australian Shepherd and a Poodle could choose to mate them, potentially resulting in Aussiedoodle puppies for sale. However, there is much more to responsible breeding than simply allowing two dogs to reproduce. Failure to do the due diligence via stringent health testing, appropriate rearing, and early socialization, can result in puppies who are not sound in health, conformation, or temperament.

A great resource for families looking to add an Aussiedoodle to their home is the International Designer Canine Registry (IDCR). IDCR is an organization which acts as a registry for hybrid breeds. This registry offers their services to breeders around the globe, giving you access to the most comprehensive list of Aussiedoodle breeders stored in one location. IDCR sees their role as a registry service which offers full registration privileges to hybrids and designer dogs. Breeders who opt to use IDCR for their registry service also gain access to their pedigree tracking software. IDCR offers a list of registered breeders to the public, making it an invaluable first stop for anyone trying to source an Aussiedoodle breeder in their area.

In addition to the IDCR, there is also an organization known as the National Hybrid Registry (NHR). In order for a crossbreed litter to be registered with NHR, breeders are first required to provide proof that the offspring were produced from two purebred parents.

If you live in the UK and are on the hunt for your perfect Aussiedoodle companion, the best place to contact is a group called Designer Dogs-The Kennel Club. The mandate of DDCR is to unite dog seekers with dog breeders. The DDCR is a UK-based registration service that registers both purebred and crossbreed dogs.

*You will need to find a reputable breeder from
which to purchase your Aussiedoodle puppy.*

Aussiedoodle Puppies for Sale—What Should You Look for?

When searching for your Aussiedoodle puppy, there are some things you should look for and some things that you should avoid. Once a breed gains popularity, disreputable people intent only on making money begin to mass produce that particular type of puppy. These operations are often referred to as "puppy mills" or even "commercial breeders." Puppy mills are known to produce and spread disease due to the inhumane conditions their breeding dogs are housed in. Not concerned with health testing or even basic veterinary care for their breeding stock, the dogs of these commercial breeders are often kept in wire cages too small to provide room to move. The dogs are often left to sit in their own feces and urine and are known to be ridden with sores and other diseases. Never receiving veterinary care, many of these dogs become gravely ill and are simply destroyed when they are no longer able to make money for their owners. Sadly, these dogs have never known love, and most have never experienced the joy of running on grass, eating high-quality food, or playing with a toy. The deaths of these poor creatures are far less than humane. Many are simply sold to be used as laboratory animals or left by the side of the road to fend for themselves. Not only is buying a puppy from such an organization a great risk given that your puppy will have been exposed to dirty, disease-ridden bedding and property but to purchase from such a breeder feeds this heartbreaking problem.

But puppy mill puppies are not just found on private properties. Many of them are also sold in local pet stores. Most often the puppies are removed from their mothers as early as four weeks of age, a time when a puppy should be learning its most critical lessons from its mother. Missing out on these crucial weeks of socialization stunts a puppy's emotional and social development. These early lessons cannot be replicated in any other way, or by any other means. Thus puppies taken from their mother this early will struggle to adapt to new environments and experiences, and many will develop intense fears and reactive behavior. It is during these first eight weeks of life that the mother dog teaches her babies how to be "dogs." To miss out on these important weeks creates a social deficit that can never be bridged.

Another puppy buying venue to avoid is online marketplaces. Many online marketplaces advertise puppies that have been bred by unscrupulous breeders who have not done their due diligence in caring for the mother or the pups that they have bred. Beware of a bargain! If the price of a puppy seems too good to be true, it most likely is! Always remember that a bargain price up front may cost you untold thousands in medical costs later.

If you discover a breeder who seems to always have Aussiedoodle puppies available, it is best to continue your search. Puppies take a great deal of time and energy to raise appropriately and socialize well. Breeders who advertise puppies for sale year-round may be commercial operations and breeding far too frequently for it to be healthy for the life of their breeding stock. Typically, ethical breeders only plan two to three litters per year as a maximum and almost always have homes waiting for their pups before they are born. In addition to this, female breeding dogs should be bred only a few times in their lives before being "retired." If you find a breeder, who has repeatedly bred their females, and especially if these girls do not experience any rest periods between litters, RUN!

Bear in mind that in order to obtain an Aussiedoodle puppy from a reputable breeder, it may be necessary to add your name to a waiting list. Depending on the demand for the breed in your area, the list could be as short as six months or as long as several years. Waiting lists give you the assurance that the breeder produces high-quality puppies that other people see as worth the wait. It is typically evidence of an excellent reputation for producing healthy, happy puppies.

So, what should you look for in an Aussiedoodle puppy?

When seeking the ideal Aussiedoodle puppy for your family, one of the first things you will want to consider is which sex you feel would be best suited to your home. Some families have strong feelings on this issue, so it is important to decide ahead of time whether or not the lucky puppy to join your home is going to be a boy or a girl. You will discover that some breeders are willing to take requests for one sex over another but prefer to match each puppy to their new families themselves. While some families long for the opportunity to choose which puppy they bring home on their own, there is a lot of wisdom in allowing the breeder to make this selection for you. If you have selected a reputable breeder to purchase your Aussiedoodle puppy from, you will soon discover that your breeder knows each puppy and its personality exceptionally well. After all, they have had eight weeks to get to know each of them, so they are the best equipped to determine which puppy will make the perfect fit in each family.

In your quest for your Aussiedoodle bundle of joy, you will also want to consider personality. Be sure to visit your breeder of choice to observe the litter at play. If you are a more laidback family with a moderate lifestyle, you won't want to bring home the puppy that is bouncing off the walls and that rarely sleeps! Even as young as six to eight weeks of age, puppies will begin to exhibit permanent personality characteristics. The shy puppy retreating into the corner may require a lot of extra socialization and training to learn to come out of its shell. These are all important things to take into consideration when selecting the right puppy for you.

While you are visiting your breeder's home, it is always a good idea to ask to see your puppy's parents. Why is that? Viewing the parents will give you an idea as to what you can expect your puppy to look like as an adult dog. This is a slightly more complex project when you are dealing with a crossbreed, but try to imagine a happy medium between the two dogs you are looking at, and you will get a general idea of what you might see when your dog reaches full maturity. You will also want to observe the parent dogs' personalities. Temperament can be formed by environment, but it is largely genetic. This is why aggressive dogs or dogs that exhibit unstable behavior should never be bred. These traits are inherited.

An important thing to bear in mind is that not all breeders will have both parents on the premises. In many cases, breeders own only the female dog and pay a stud fee to the male dog's owner in return for his "services." Under these circumstances, the breeder should be able to show you photos, health clearances, and the dog's pedigree, and should you so desire, they should also be able to put you in touch with the stud dog owner in case you want to go to meet them and their dog as well.

Another important thing to ask your breeder is to see health clearances. Prior to being bred, both the Australian Shepherd and the Poodle should be health tested for every possible genetic and physical disease that is common to both breeds. To produce healthy puppies, it takes two healthy animals. If you request to see health testing results from a breeder and the breeder is reluctant to share them, or does not have them, run! Reputable breeders ALWAYS health test and are only too happy to share their dogs' results when asked.

If possible, try to take the opportunity to see where your puppy was born and the area in which it was raised. Understanding where your puppy got its start in life and what early experiences it underwent will give you great insight into the delightful creature you are about to bring home with you! But also, a breeder's home, whelping area, and puppy rooms should be kept clean, neat, and organized. Any signs of obvious neglect should be cause for concern for you.

Puppies should leave the nest for their new homes no sooner than eight weeks. For some breeders, ten weeks is preferable, and a rare few will hang on to their pups until 12 weeks. Under no circumstances should a puppy ever leave its home prior to eight weeks of age. If a breeder offers you this option, they are not the breeder for you. What is best for your puppy is ultimately what is best for you. No matter how hard it is to wait until its eight-week-old birthday, you will be glad that you did!

Important Questions to Ask Aussiedoodle Breeders

Choosing a puppy is a little like hiring someone for a job. You want to take the time to do your research and to ask the right questions to select just the right person from which to purchase your Aussiedoodle puppy. Taking the time to be thorough will reap the rewards in spades!

Be aware that most reputable breeders will want to grill you as much as you want to grill them, and they will not mind being asked sincere questions about their puppies or their breeding and rearing practices. After all, you are both looking for the perfect fit! Reputable breeders do not sell their puppies to just anyone. Many will require you to fill out a detailed puppy application as a pre-screening ritual. This process allows the breeder to get to know you and your family a little better as well as to assess your suitability to the breed. Often, you will be asked to make a visit to the breeder's home for the opportunity to meet them and the puppies in person and to continue the interview process prior to being granted approval to purchase a puppy.

There are several important questions to ask a breeder you are considering purchasing your Aussiedoodle puppy from.

- **May I see the puppy's parents?**

  As previously discussed, viewing the puppy's parents in their home environment will allow you to get a better idea as to what your puppy may look like when it reaches maturity. This is a great time to assess personality strengths and coat condition as well.

- **What are your methods for socialization?**

  It is important for you to understand how the breeder introduced the puppy to its new experiences. Has the puppy met other dogs? Cats? How many new people have the puppy met? Are there any particular socialization protocols the breeder follows, such as Puppy Culture or Dr. Carmen Battaglia's Early Neurological Stimulation? All of this is important information for you to understand how your puppy has been raised.

- **Has the puppy been vaccinated and dewormed, and at what age?**

  Most breeders will give you a detailed health record, including all dewormings and vaccinations. You should also be given a schedule for all follow-up vaccinations in the puppy series.

- **What food do you recommend for the puppy?**

  Puppies have very sensitive stomachs. Transitioning to any new food must be done very gradually and always with mixing in some of the old food and over time phasing it out until only the new food remains. With this in mind, it is important to understand what your puppy is currently eating. Most breeders will send home a small bag of the food the puppy has been eating with recommendations for amounts and any food changes that may be necessary as the puppy grows.

- **May I see the health clearances for each parent?**

  It always pays to know ahead of time what genetic and physical diseases Poodles and Australian Shepherds are predisposed to. This will make it easier to discuss this topic with a breeder and to understand what you should be looking for. Since hip dysplasia is the most common health ailment experienced by Aussiedoodles to date, it will be important for you to ask the breeder to see OFA (Orthopedic Foundation for Animals) hip results, to ensure the parents of your puppy had hip scores in the "Normal" range. Common health problems and appropriate screening for breeding will be more thoroughly explored in other chapters.

- **Are there any known diseases in the lines of either parent?**

  Sometimes health problems may not be present in the parents but linger in dogs further back in the pedigree. It is worth asking the breeder if there are any known illnesses, diseases, or conditions in their bloodlines. It could be that a grandfather had a heart murmur or a great great grandmother had poor patellas (knees). This is all valuable information to have. It does not mean these problems will befall your dog, and it is particularly unlikely if the ailments are several generations removed. But the more information you can gather, the clearer the picture you will get of your puppy's heritage.

- **Will the puppy come with a contract and a health guarantee? What is the health guarantee?**

  Most breeders do have a contract. This contract clearly stipulates what is expected of you and what the breeder offers you in return. You will want to read this carefully and ask questions to be sure you are prepared to fulfill your end of the contract and that you are comfortable with what the breeder will extend to you as the puppy's owner. In addition to this, each breeder should offer you some form of a health guarantee. While it is unrealistic to expect any breeder would guarantee a puppy will remain healthy for its entire life, many offer a lifetime guarantee against certain inherited diseases, others will offer a limited guarantee on certain items, and others still will offer conditional guarantees based on obligations you must fulfill, otherwise the guarantee will be voided.

- **At what age can the puppy go to its new home?**

  You are looking for a very specific answer to this question. If the breeder allows their puppies to leave their home any earlier than eight weeks of age, it's time to look for another breeder.

- **What is your return policy?**

  No one goes into a venture like this thinking they will return their puppy. However, life is messy, and it's important to know what is supposed to happen in the event you can't keep your puppy. Divorce, life-altering illness, deaths in the family---all of these situations can leave you unable to care for a dog; no matter how much you might love it. The vast majority of breeders will have a clause in their contracts stating that if you can no longer keep the dog, for any reason, that the dog is to come home to the breeder. Many also offer large financial penalties against any owner who rehomes the dog or places it in a shelter or rescue organization.

What Can You Expect to Pay for an Aussiedoodle?

Since dog breeding is not regulated by any particular industry that standardizes prices, you will find that prices for Aussiedoodle puppies are subject to the laws of supply and demand. Prices will fluctuate greatly from breeder to breeder and will also be different depending on where you happen to live. Always remember that the bargain-priced puppy truly is no bargain in the long run.

Aussiedoodles are an extremely popular designer dog breed at this time. Unfortunately, this means that you will pay more for your puppy than you would to obtain a different breed. Though you may find some puppies priced as low as $700 (540 GBP), the average price for an Aussiedoodle puppy rings in around $1,200 (920 GBP) and can range as high as $2,800 (2,200 GBP).

Buying an Adult Aussiedoodle—What Must You Consider?

Buying an adult dog is always a different venture from buying a puppy. Sometimes breeders will "retire" an adult dog from their breeding program, meaning a fully trained adult Aussiedoodle may become available to you. Adults have their advantages and disadvantages. Yes, you will miss the cute puppy years, but you also gain a dog with the life experience to integrate well into family living, with minimal adjustment. In addition to this, an adult Aussiedoodle will already come to you house trained, saving you tons of work and ruined rugs!

Most adult Aussiedoodles are found in rescues. While ending up in a rescue is often no fault of the dog itself, it can mean that you will have added training challenges to deal with, to help your dog learn to adapt to life in its new home. This is not necessarily a deterrent. Some of the best family pets are found in rescues and shelters, and these dogs are definitely worth consideration!

When considering an adult Aussiedoodle, you will want to ask a lot of the same questions you asked when seeking to purchase an Aussiedoodle puppy from a breeder. If you can obtain a thorough health history of the dog, it will be very helpful for you. Adult Aussiedoodles, whether they are sourced from rescues, shelters, or a breeder, will all come with vaccination records and a health report, so you have a better understanding of what your next steps should be in protecting your dog's health.

Adult Aussiedoodles are also more likely to have "settled." This settling means a less exuberant dog which often translates to one with better canine manners. In a sense, it's like obtaining a pre-trained dog. You get all of the benefits without having to put in the work!

CHAPTER 5

Aussiedoodle Adoption— Adopting an Aussiedoodle Puppy or Adult Dog

A dopting an Aussiedoodle puppy or adult dog is a great idea. With so many dogs in shelters needing great homes, adopting from a rescue allows you to give a dog a second chance at a great life. Shelter dogs often end up in rescue through no fault of their own. If you're determined the Aussiedoodle is the breed for you, it is a great idea to stop by your local shelter or rescue to see if the perfect pup or adult dog is just waiting to join your family!

Rescue Aussiedoodles love to have fun too!

Understanding a Rescue Aussiedoodle's Past

It is important to realize that your rescue Aussiedoodle has a past, and that past will affect how it views the world. When you first adopt your Aussiedoodle puppy or adult dog, you will need to be patient. It will take time for your dog to acclimate to its new environment, and the behavior you see early on is not necessarily a true picture of what your dog will be like once it feels "at home."

Rescued Aussiedoodles—Special Care

Aussiedoodles who have come from rescues require lots of patience and the opportunity to come out of their shell when ready to do so. You may notice some setbacks in things like basic manners and housetraining. It is always wise to remember that your Aussiedoodle is just learning where things are in your home and what the process is to let you know that it needs to go outside to use the bathroom. These things will come with time.

Don't force your Aussiedoodle to do things that it is not yet comfortable with. By the same token, don't be alarmed if your new dog doesn't want to cuddle up to you just yet or prefers to sleep on the floor than in the new comfortable bed you just purchased. For some dogs, it will take time to build the confidence to get close to people again and to try new things. Your patience and love will be greatly rewarded in due time.

Reputable Aussiedoodle Rescues

Though there are no known Aussiedoodle-specific rescues to date, although you may be able to find Aussiedoodles in need of a home through a variety of different avenues. Rescue organizations that deal with all breeds of dogs may end up with an Aussiedoodle in care, from time to time. Should you have your heart set on this wonderful breed, you could always contact a few reputable rescues to let them know, that should one be taken into their rescue, you would be very interested in being contacted. This same approach can also work for your local shelter. Simply leave your name and number and ask them to give you a call, should an Aussiedoodle become available.

Breeders are also an excellent networking tool for Aussiedoodles in need of rehoming. Since the breed is relatively new and not yet as popular as some purebreds, most Aussiedoodle breeders within a region are familiar with one another, and they work collaboratively to help find homes for Aussiedoodles who are no longer able to stay with their original families. This could also be a wonderful resource for you. Contact reputable breeders in your area to let them know of your interest in the breed and ask to be kept notified if any come available for adoption. This will keep you in the loop for the future.

Online resources are also available to you via companies such as Petfinder who unite people looking for a specific breed with dogs of that breed found within a designated zone.

Finding Aussiedoodles for Adoption Near Me

The best resource for finding Aussiedoodles in need of a home is an internet search. There are many different online web portals which list specific dog breeds for rehoming. Sometimes online marketplaces will also list private sellers wanting to place their dog with a new family. Though this could potentially work out to be a good situation for you and for the dog, you need to be very careful when considering a dog offered online to a new home. You will want to be sure to see up-to-date health and vaccination records, as well as to observe the dog in its home environment. These few things will tell you a bit about the dog's history and what behavior you can likely expect in your home. This is especially important if you have children or other animals. As much as you may long to help an animal in need, not every home is equipped to deal with a dog with severe behavioral issues or medical needs. You want the current owners to be as upfront with you as possible, so you truly understand what you are committing to.

Giving Back—Volunteering with an Aussiedoodle Rescue

Though at present there are no organized Aussiedoodle rescue organizations, you can help out Aussiedoodles who do come into care in an all-breed rescue or shelter, by volunteering. Rescues and shelters aren't choosy about how many hours you work or what skills you have to offer; they are just grateful for another set of hands and a willing heart. If you have a specific talent, you can be of great assistance by suggesting ways that you could use that to help raise funds for a rescue, or to assist with a project.

You could also simply volunteer your time to walk dogs at your local shelter. With so many dogs needing exercise, an extra dog walker is a blessing indeed!

Even something as simple as donating needed supplies such as paper towel, cleaning supplies, dog beds, dog toys, dog food, etc. is an invaluable help. Shelters and rescues often run on very limited budgets, so any gift, no matter how small, is always appreciated.

CHAPTER 6

Aussiedoodle Supplies— What Do You Need?

O nce you have found the right breeder and have a date when you can pick up your Aussiedoodle puppy, you will need to get stocked up on supplies. Puppies need all kinds of different things. Some will need to be purchased in advance of your Aussiedoodle pup's arrival, while other items should wait until your pup can tag along on the shopping trip too. Your breeder will likely have helpful tips and suggestions that you should consider when preparing for your Aussiedoodle puppy to arrive. Aussiedoodle breeders have specialized knowledge of the breed and its unique needs and are an excellent resource for you when you have questions.

*Your Aussiedoodle will need lots of supplies to keep it healthy,
well-groomed, and strong.*

Aussiedoodle Food—What is the Best Food and Where Do You Find It?

When it comes to what food to feed your Aussiedoodle pup, you will find that there are differing opinions. The best place to start is by asking your breeder for advice. Generally, it is always best to continue feeding your puppy the food your breeder has started the pup on. Your Aussiedoodle pup will experience a lot of changes in the first few days after leaving the breeder's home; you don't want to introduce something else that might cause your pup additional stress. Puppies need time to adapt from what they are currently eating to a new food, and it is never a good idea to make a change in food "cold turkey." Moving from the old food directly to the new food is a recipe for an upset tummy which will often be accompanied by very loose stools, and possibly vomiting as well. If you do opt to change your Aussiedoodle puppy's food, you will want to be sure to do it gradually. Experts typically recommend that you begin by mixing the old food with the new food at a ratio of 1:1. Over time, you can gradually reduce the amount of old food until all that remains is the new food. Allow your puppy's bowel movements to serve as your guide. In general, the entire process should take approximately a week, to a week and a half. It is always best to proceed cautiously, to allow your puppy's developing digestive system time to process a dietary change.

Though it is always recommended that you continue with what your breeder has been feeding for a time, it is important to consider the unique needs of a puppy if you opt to change to a different brand of food. Recent research shows that foods that are comprised of greater than 20 percent protein and/or supplemented with additional calcium may lead to rapid bone growth. While this would seem to be a wonderful thing for a puppy, it actually can cause developmental problems. Though the bone is quick to respond to the nutrition it is receiving, muscle continues to grow at the same rate, meaning your puppy's systems are developing differently. This can lead to future structural problems. For this reason, it is always recommended that you choose a puppy food that contains no more than 20 percent protein from the highest quality protein sources such as chicken, beef, lamb, whitefish, salmon, rabbit, kangaroo, venison, turkey, duck, or pork.

You will also want to bear in mind that puppies are highly individual. Even dogs born in the same litter may do best on entirely different foods. In addition to this, some breeds are more prone to skin conditions and allergies than others, making them more sensitive to food and treats. The Aussiedoodle is not known to be a breed that suffers from allergies, so this is one less consideration you will have to factor into your decision.

The Aussiedoodle is a high energy breed, and thus, you will want to source a puppy food that will be up to the task of providing high-quality nutrition and sufficient calories to power your puppy. To this end; bear in mind, that size matters. Your Aussiedoodle is a medium-sized puppy and will become a medium-sized dog. You won't want to purchase small breed puppy food for your Aussiedoodle, as it may not contain sufficient calories to meet your puppy's daily needs. In addition to this, the amount of calcium and phosphorous necessary for correct bone growth is scaled accordingly in puppy food for small breeds and for large breeds. You want to be certain the formulation you select has the correct ratios for your size of puppy.

Typically, with puppies, you want to feed smaller meals more frequently throughout the day. This will allow for an even distribution of daily calories to meet your Aussiedoodle's energy needs.

When choosing a food for your puppy, it is typically best to choose a puppy food over an adult food, though some companies do offer an "all stages" blend, which would provide suitable nutrition for your dog. You would not, however, want to purchase adult food for your puppy. Adult food contains fewer calories than a puppy needs to properly develop and grow.

Another consideration to keep in mind when purchasing a kibble is the size of each individual piece of food in the brand you are considering. Small breed formulations are often made in tiny pieces which are not suitable for a medium to large-sized puppy.

You may also find that if you purchase this type of food, your puppy will become frustrated at how long it takes to eat it and may try to wolf it down rapidly causing pieces to get caught in its throat. For this reason, tiny kibble pieces can be a choking hazard to medium to large size puppies. If you read the label of the food you are considering, it will tell you if the formulation is for small or large breeds. Avoid small breed food for your Aussiedoodle puppy.

The quality of the food you choose to feed your Aussiedoodle puppy will affect its overall health and can affect your puppy's growth as well. Choose a high quality, nutritious food that is properly balanced. Taking time to carefully read labels will assist you in choosing a food that is best suited to your puppy's needs. Avoid foods whose ingredients list use the word "by-products" as one or more of the first ingredients. If possible, you want to select a food that has an ingredients list you recognize and understand. Typically, these foods will cost you more money than the average grocery store brands, and there is a reason for it. Premium foods contain high-quality ingredients and don't bulk up on fillers, meaning your dog gets the maximum nutrition for your dollar. Foods whose lists contain multiple chemicals or unusual sounding names you don't recognize are best avoided. When in doubt, it is always an excellent idea to consult your veterinarian who can provide recommendations as to healthy foods for your puppy and its stage of life.

So, where do you find this food? Typically, foods sold in grocery stores are the lowest common denominator on the food chain and are best avoided. Premium foods can be purchased through high-quality pet retailers as well as online. Many veterinary clinics also sell foods, including prescription diets for specific needs.

In today's canine community, raw and cooked diets have also gained popularity. While these types of food can be healthy and nutritious for your puppy, they must be properly balanced with correct vitamins, minerals, and supplements, and prepared with the utmost of care and attention to proper food safety practices. This should never be attempted without a proper recipe which has been approved by your veterinarian.

The bottom line is to choose the best quality food that your budget will allow. Even if you cannot afford to buy the most expensive brand on the shelf, there are lots of more moderately priced foods that are also excellent choices for your Aussiedoodle. Read labels carefully, do your research, and let your budget be your final guide, and you can't go wrong!

Aussiedoodle Beds—What is the Most Comfortable Bedding for Your Aussiedoodle?

When you bring your new Aussiedoodle pooch home, you're going to need a comfortable place for it to rest. Decide ahead of time if your puppy will be permitted to lay on your furniture and bed. Making these decisions ahead of time will help you with training, an important consideration since puppies need consistency to learn well.

As a dog that will grow to medium size, the biggest thing you will need to take into account when looking at bedding for your Aussiedoodle is size. Though a small dog bed might suit your puppy to a T, always remember that your puppy will grow. The bed that once fit perfectly will no longer have a use when your adult Aussiedoodle becomes too big to fit in it! When you go shopping for the perfect bed for your puppy, select a bed that your dog can grow into. Most dogs do not mind a bed that is larger than their current size, but none of them will want to lay in one that is too small.

There are many different styles of beds to choose from. Most dogs aren't too picky and will lay wherever is softest and most convenient.

Here is a list of some of the most popular dog bed styles available today:

- **Orthopedic beds**

  Orthopedic beds often come with a layer of mattress to provide support for your dog's bones and joints. Though most typically purchased for older dogs, orthopedic beds are still an excellent choice for puppies as well. They are generally made of sturdy construction, meaning they will stand up to regular wear and tear well.

- **Cave beds**

  One of the newest styles of dog beds on the market today, cave beds are quickly becoming a staple in the homes of most dog owners. Since many dogs love to burrow inside their beds to have their entire body covered, cave beds afford them the option of indulging their primal instincts which are a throwback to their days as canines in the wild. Cave beds typically resemble an open-faced hard taco. Your dog simply climbs inside and snuggles in for a rest or nap. Most are covered in soft fleece or velour and are lined with synthetic sheepskin for the ultimate in comfort. Most cave bed covers are fully removable for washing; however, they can prove a challenge to get back on, once removed.

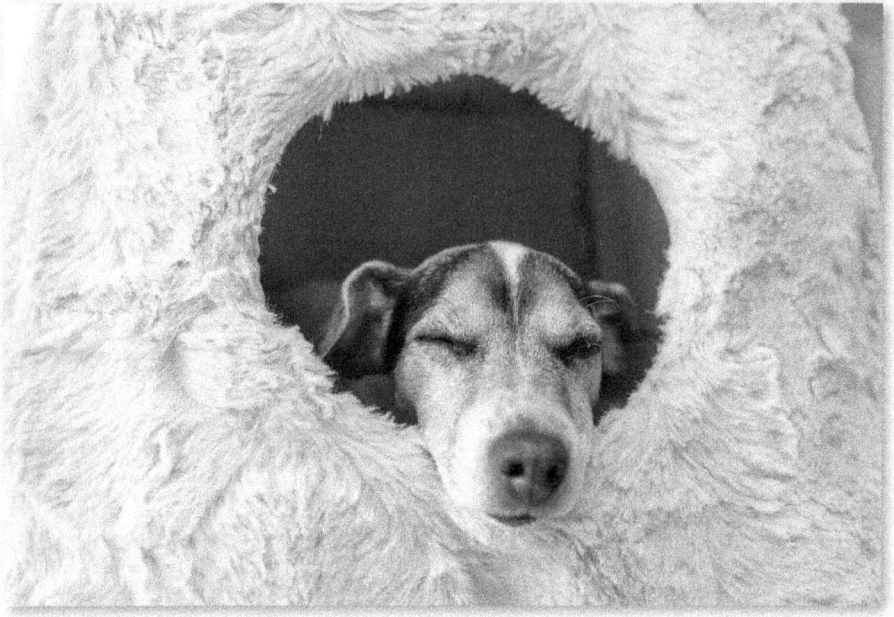

Aussiedoodles love to rest in cave beds just like this one!

- **Heated beds**

    Since heat can often provide a soothing balm for aching canine joints as well as take the edge off cold winter nights, some dog bed manufacturers have created versions of their standard donut style beds that are equipped with heaters sure to keep your Aussiedoodle puppy toasty warm! The only potential downside to purchasing a heated bed for your puppy is that is must be plugged in, meaning the bed must be placed near to an outlet. As an added concern, your puppy may find the cord too much temptation to resist! If you suspect this may be the case, you might be best to delay using a heated bed until your puppy has learned to restrict its chewing to more appropriate items, such as toys and bones.

- **Kuranda or elevated beds**

  Kuranda, or elevated beds, are many dogs preferred type of bedding. These typically consist of an elevated piece of canvas stretched over a footed frame comprised of PVC pipe. Most dogs find them extremely comfortable, and they are ideal for using outdoors. Kuranda beds are easy to clean. Just grab a cloth and some pet safe disinfectant, spray the bed down, give it a good wipe, and you are good to go!

- **Donut beds**

  If you've ever watched a dog circling and circling and circling before curling up into a ball and plopping into place, you know that dogs love the donut position! A donut bed is essentially a round cushion with an indented center, providing the ideal spot for your dog to relax in its favorite position. Available in several different sizes, these beds are most often better suited to smaller dogs, making them an excellent choice for a puppy, but perhaps not so much for your adult Aussiedoodle. Fortunately, they are available at quite low price points, allowing you the opportunity to purchase one or two for the puppy years, that you can later replace, as your pup grows.

- **Bolster-style beds**

  The bolster-style bed is similar to the donut bed. Instead of being circular and containing an indentation in the center, the bolster bed is usually rectangular and contains "bolsters" along the back and sides to provide a spot for your dog to rest its head. Bolster beds are particularly comfortable for medium-sized to large breed dogs, making them an excellent choice for an Aussiedoodle.

- **Large pillow beds**

  One of the simplest and most comfortable beds you will find is a pillow bed. Available in many sizes, you are sure to find one that is the perfect fit for your Aussiedoodle puppy.

Some important considerations:

Puppies can be quite mischievous and love to explore their world with their teeth. The Aussiedoodle is no exception to this rule! With this in mind, here are a few important things that you will need to consider as you shop for the ideal bed for your Aussiedoodle puppy:

- **Is the bed durable enough to withstand puppy teeth?**

  Make no mistake, puppies WILL chew their new bed. With this in mind, a bargain-priced bed may be no bargain. If your pup has a penchant for destroying anything plush, you won't want to invest a lot of money in a bed. In this case, you would be wise to choose a donut or pillow style bed as they are cost-effective and easily replaced if your pup decides to do its worst damage on it. Until your pup can be trusted not to chew cords, it is best to avoid a heated bed.

- **Does the bed have a removable cover for washing?**

  Puppies have accidents during the housebreaking process, and these accidents will sometimes happen on your puppy's bed. Unless you are the proud owner of a washing machine with an exceptionally large drum or don't mind frequenting your local Laundromat, you will be out of luck if you purchase a bed that does not have a removable cover. For ease of cleaning, always check to be certain the bed you are considering has covers which zip on and off. This simple feature will make your life much easier and will make keeping your puppy's bedding April fresh a breeze.

Aussiedoodle Collars—How Do You Get the Right Fit?

Every puppy needs a collar, and the Aussiedoodle is no exception. The most important thing in selecting the correct collar to be certain of the right fit. Collars that are too tight can choke your dog or become embedded in their skin, causing irritation, rashes, cuts, and pain. Yet collars that are too loose allow your dog the freedom to slip its head out should the dog so desire. The last thing you need is a puppy on the run! A correct fit is critical to the safety of your dog.

Bear in mind that your Aussiedoodle is going to grow, so the first collar you buy for your puppy is certainly not the last one you will ever purchase. With this in mind, you may want to opt to avoid the more expensive leather collars and instead proceed directly to something in nylon. These types of collars are often available in bright colors and prints to allow you to customize your choice to your dog's specific personality and gender.

To ensure a correct fit for your Aussiedoodle puppy, you should bring the dog with you to the store. The only way to know for sure if the collar will properly do its job is to measure it on the dog that will be wearing it. Though most collars do come in standard sizes with a list of suggested breeds it may fit, each dog is an individual and what may fit your friend's Aussiedoodle puppy might not fit yours.

As a general rule of thumb, a collar fits correctly if you can slip two of your fingers underneath it without it becoming too tight and causing your puppy to choke. Any more than that, and it is too big. Conversely, if you can't get both fingers underneath the band, it is far too small.

Aussiedoodle Leashes—How Do You Choose a Style and Length?

The correct leash for your Aussiedoodle will depend on your dog's age and what you plan to use the leash for. For puppies, it is typically best to limit your leash length to six feet. A six-foot lead constructed of leather or nylon is what is most typically used for obedience training. Whether you opt to learn basic manners or to advance on to competitive obedience, a six-foot lead is the tool you will need. A six-foot lead gives your dog ample room to explore its surroundings but is short enough for it to focus on you. It is the perfect tool for mastering the heel command, an important skill that every dog should learn.

There are longer leads available which are ideal for training your Aussiedoodle puppy the recall command. Leashes of 12 feet or longer give your dog the freedom to roam further away from you to explore their world but offer you the security that the dog is still attached to you via a tether.

A flexible lead is another type of leash that can prove useful. If your puppy is not trustworthy off-lead but needs more room to roam, a flexible lead can be the perfect solution. Flexible leads range in retractable lengths from 16 feet to up to 26 feet. They are best used in a controlled setting such as a field. Simply stand in place with the flexible lead in your hand and allow your dog the full length of the retractable lead to race around and have a ball. It is a great way for your dog to burn off some steam in a safe fashion. Flexible leads are not good tools for use in dog parks or on dog walks. Although they do come equipped with the ability to "halt" the lead at your desired length via a locking system, the lock can sometimes be triggered to loosen, inadvertently allowing your dog the full length of the leash when you least want your dog having access to it. In addition to this, many owners panic when they spy a dog heading their way and attempt to grab the cord or tape and end up severely cutting or burning their hands. For this reason, the flexible lead is a tool best used only in safe environments for the purpose of giving your dog some added exercise.

Aussiedoodle Harnesses—Is a Harness a Good Choice for an Aussiedoodle?

A harness can be an excellent choice for your Aussiedoodle. Since this breed is well known for their exuberance and excitability, it is quite likely your Aussiedoodle will like to pull, especially when it is just learning to walk on a lead. If you opt to use a collar, you run the risk of your Aussiedoodle putting pressure on its trachea, causing choking and potentially permanent damage.

A harness is a great alternative to collars. You can purchase some which allow for a leash to be hooked in the middle of the back or at the very front. The ideal harness must fit properly in order to be effective. If it is too tight, it will rub and cause painful lesions and skin irritation on your dog. If it is too loose, your Aussiedoodle may easily be able to slip out of it. As with collars, the best way to ensure you have the correct fit is by taking your dog to the store with you. An assistant can assist you in selecting the correct size.

While you are shopping for the ideal harness, take time to consider different styles. Harnesses can put extra strain across your dog's back and shoulders if your dog is prone to pulling. A front clip harness might be a better solution in this case.

Aussiedoodle Kennels—How Do You Select the Right Size?

A dog crate or kennel is essential in most homes. Many owners use them to assist with housetraining. Since many breeders begin crate training while the puppies are as young as five weeks old, many puppies associate crates or kennels as being comfortable places to take a nap. This type of training is always helpful as it will be necessary at times in your Aussiedoodle's life for it to spend time in a crate. Whether a kennel becomes your dog's bed, a convenient place to stay when you can't be home to supervise, or a means of containment when traveling in your car, it is a useful skill for your dog to see its crate as a safe and happy place to be. At the very least, a time will come when your dog needs to visit the vet, and a short respite in one of their kennels might be necessary. You can take the worry and fear out of such a stay now by teaching your Aussiedoodle that kennels are a great place to be!

If your dog ever needs to travel by airplane, it will be necessary for it to travel in a crate. Since Aussiedoodles are too large to travel in the cabin with their owners, they must travel in the cargo hold. Following the specifications for airline travel is very helpful in determining what size crate is appropriate for your dog. Typically, airlines require that the kennel be large enough for your dog to stand up, turn around, and lay back down comfortably. A headspace of two inches to four inches is preferable.

Care must be taken that the kennel is not too large. If you make use of a crate when transporting your dog in your vehicle, a crate that is too big for your dog subjects it to excess jostling, which can cause serious injury to your dog if a collision were to occur.

Aussiedoodle Dog Houses—How Do You Choose a Size and What Features Do You Need?

Since Aussiedoodles are a breed which thrives on close proximity to their people, it is not advised that your dog lives outdoors. However, providing a safe haven where your dog can retreat during inclement weather should it so choose, is always a great idea.

Today's dog houses come in a variety of different sizes and styles. Many quality manufacturers will customize your dog house to look like a smaller version of your home. Ideally, your Aussiedoodle's dog house should be something that remains clean and dry on the inside. The purpose of a dog house is to provide shelter when the outdoor elements are far less than favorable. Though a doghouse does not need to have the same headspace as a crate, you will want to be sure that your dog can easily get inside the house with a minimal amount of ducking and that that they can easily turn around and lay down.

You can line your Aussiedoodle's dog house with comfortable, absorbent bedding or straw or hay, though the latter two mediums will provide some insulation, but not as much comfort. If you opt to make use of bedding, you will need to check it daily and wash it as frequently as is necessary, to keep it dry, clean, and smelling fresh.

Many companies also make heating pads that can be placed in a dog house to keep your Aussiedoodle warm when the weather isn't so nice out.

Aussiedoodle Toys—What Selection Should You Make to Keep Your Dog Stimulated?

Providing appropriate physical and mental stimulation for your Aussiedoodle is the key to keeping it content. Aussiedoodles are a highly intelligent breed with energy to spare. If your dog does not have access to toys that allow it to exercise its brain and its jaws, it may become prone to nuisance behaviors.

Variety is the key to keeping your dog mentally and physically satisfied. The best way to achieve this is by purchasing toys in as many different shapes, sizes, colors, and textures as possible. But many owners make the mistake of throwing all of their purchased toys into one toy box and assuming that should be enough to keep their dog out of trouble. Dogs tire of the same toys just as we tire of eating the same foods on a regular basis. The simplest way to avoid this is by rotating your dog's toy supply. Include a few different items for your Aussiedoodle to enjoy on Monday. On Tuesday, take a few out and replace them with something new. Continue this pattern all week to keep your Aussiedoodle's interest piqued.

Toys for your Aussiedoodle do not necessarily need to be expensive ones from your favorite pet store. By all means, purchase some of those, but you can round them out with things like rubber toys suitable for stuffing with something tasty then frozen to provide maximum licking pleasure or toilet paper rolls with treats inside and the ends folded over and taped shut…a handmade puzzle for your dog to unravel.

Commercial puzzle toys such as treat balls, are another great item to include in your toy box. These types of toys reward your dog for their determination to solve the puzzle. What could be more fun?

Of course, when purchasing toys, there are a few considerations you must keep in mind. Be certain to select toys that are high quality and up to the task of withstanding the chewing strength of your Aussiedoodle. Toys that are easily torn apart may end up swallowed, causing painful obstructions or choking hazards. By the same token, be sure to choose toys that are the appropriate size for your dog and that are intended for dog use. This simple safety precaution could save your dog's life.

Aussiedoodle Dog Treats—How Do You Choose Safe and Yummy Snacks for Your Aussiedoodle?

Your Aussiedoodle will likely eat nearly everything, but not everything is meant to be eaten by your dog! Choosing safe and yummy snacks can be a challenge. There are so many treats on the market today; it can be very difficult to make a selection you can feel good about.

Some of the most popular treats housed at eye level at your favorite pet store are ones that are best avoided. Though your Aussiedoodle may devour them with delight, many of them have less than helpful effects on your dog's health.

Some of the treats best left on the shelf are:

* **Rawhides**

   Though dogs love rawhides, rawhides are treated to harsh chemical solutions in order to shape hide into shelf-stable chews, for canine consumption. These chemicals are most definitely harmful to our dogs, and the rawhide treat itself is not much better. To ensure the rawhide has as long a shelf life as possible, it is often treated with preservatives and antibiotics that have been known to be laced with arsenic, a type of poison!

A lesser known fact is that rawhide is difficult to digest. The same chemicals added to create a long-lasting chew make the product slow to break down in the gut. In addition to this, a swallowed piece of rawhide has the potential to swell, causing a multitude of serious stomach problems, and in some cases, even death.

- **Hooves**

  Hooves receive a similar treatment to rawhides. To be certain the product is clean enough for canines to consume, hooves are subjected to insecticides, bleaches, and other chemicals, rendering the hoof "clean" but hardly safe for your dog to chew.

  In addition to this, hooves are particularly hard and can cause your dog's teeth to chip or even break.

- **Pig's ears**

  There are few treats that get a dog salivating the way a pig's ear does! Pig's ears are high in fat, which can lead to pancreatitis, a condition which can be acute or severe in dogs, and which most often requires veterinary intervention to alleviate.

  Like both hooves and rawhides, pig's ears are subject to chemical processes to preserve them and clean them for canine use.

  Pig's ears can splinter into sharp pieces which could potentially cause painful rips or tears in your dog's throat, stomach, or mouth.

But dogs love treats, and there is no greater joy than seeing your dog enjoy something special that you bought or prepared just for them! A few general guidelines apply to learning to select appropriate treats for your dog. Be certain to choose treats which are made from ingredients that are as natural as possible. Though some preservatives may be required to keep a product from quickly spoiling, you want to purchase treats with as few additives as possible. As with choosing nutritious food, the fewer words in the ingredients list that you don't understand, the better.

In addition to this, you will need different treats for different jobs. For training purposes, you will want small, extremely high-value treats. The treats need to be small to discourage weight gain during training sessions and high value to encourage your dog to see working as fun! These treats should be reserved specifically for training times to help your dog view them as an extra special reward. They will lose their appeal if allowed to become an everyday treat.

You will also need lower value treats in your reward repertoire. Lower value treats are things that you can give to reinforce learned behaviors or whenever you just feel like giving your dog something that it enjoys because you love to do it!

Here are some safe and yummy treats you can give to your Aussiedoodle:

- **Biscuit-like treats**

    Hard biscuits take a little more chewing power, but many dogs love them. These are the ideal treats to have in your pocket on a dog walk for a quick reward, or the opportunity to train a new behavior. Because they often require more than one bite, they are not well-suited to more rigorous training sessions but are great for everyday or "just because" treats.

Today, many cookbooks exist with excellent recipes, allowing you to make your own dog treats. These often make the best biscuits, as they are free from any additives or preservatives. However, they have a low shelf life and often must be kept refrigerated.

- **Soft treats**

  Soft treats are a favorite of many Aussiedoodles. Soft treats are especially effective at helping you to teach your dog to take a treat "politely," as grabby behavior will simply cause the treat to tear or disintegrate.

  These types of treats often require refrigeration and have a limited shelf life. They are often quite fragrant and exceptionally tasty.

- **Small, training treats**

  No Aussiedoodle house is complete without small, training treats! Keep them small, so you can give as many as you like to reward your dog for good behavior or lessons learned, without fear of weight gain. Training treats should be super yummy and super smelly for best results!

  The Internet has many different recipes for things like liver cake and tuna fudge. These treats are perfect for cutting into small bite-sized pieces that are perfect for training. They will keep your Aussiedoodle extremely motivated to learn, for sure!

  For best results, choose treats that you can easily slip into a pocket, and that will not go moldy or break apart easily.

- **Dehydrated meats**

  Dogs love dehydrated meats! High-quality pet retailers sell all kinds of dehydrated meat treats. You will find you can purchase anything from beef and lamb lung to liver, tripe, and more! Find your dog's favorite and stock up, so you'll have extra special treats to surprise your Aussiedoodle, with when the mood strikes.

- **Appropriate people food**

  Though for some people food is toxic, and for some it is too high in fat for your dog to tolerate well, there are some people foods you can use for an extra special treat, on occasion. When it comes to people food, every dog is different in their tastes. Some dogs will do backflips for baby carrots and Brussels sprouts, while others reserve their best tricks for small squares of roast beef or a spoonful of mashed potatoes. If you plan to give your dog people food as a reward, always be certain the food is safe for dog consumption and feed the food only in moderation. Bear in mind that if you feed people food a little too frequently, you may inadvertently train your Aussiedoodle to be a picky eater who is not that keen on eating their dog food anymore.

Aussiedoodle Muzzles—How Do You Make Sure the Muzzle Fits?

Though muzzles have earned a stigma as being used only for aggressive dogs, muzzles do have their purpose in every dog's life, and it is to your dog's advantage for you to teach your dog that a muzzle isn't necessarily a bad thing.

Muzzles can be used for everything from reducing barking to enabling grooming, to preventing your vet from getting bitten, if your dog is experiencing intense pain. For this reason, every dog should be "shaped" to accept wearing a muzzle, when the occasion warrants it.

As with most tools such as collars and harnesses, a muzzle is only effective if it fits properly. To ensure the correct fit, follow these simple instructions:

- With your dog's mouth open at a pant, measure the distance around your dog's snout from the widest point (closest to the eyes).
- Measure the distance from the bridge of the nose to the tip. This measurement will tell you the length you require.
- Measure the height from the tip of the nose to the bottom of the jaw.

These three measurements will assist you in selecting the correct size. Armed with these measurements, you should then proceed to your local pet store. Be sure to bring your Aussiedoodle along with you as measurements provide a fairly accurate guideline, but it is always best to fit the tool on the dog that will be wearing it. Your dog should still be easily able to pant and move their mouth within reason.

There are two different styles of muzzle, and you will need to decide which one you prefer to use. One type of muzzle restricts movement so as to prevent a bite. This type of muzzle is only for use in short-term situations such as grooming routines. Called an occlusion muzzle, this style of muzzle does restrict panting, and thus, should only be used for extremely short periods of time, and always under direct supervision.

For more long-term muzzling, a basket type muzzle is preferable. The basket muzzle does not inhibit mouth movement; it simply removes access for the dog's teeth. The dog can still drink, pant, bark, and do anything it desires to do…except bite.

CHAPTER 7

Aussiedoodle Needs— How Can You Best Take Care Of Your Aussiedoodle?

E very dog has needs, and it is important to understand the unique requirements of caring for an Aussiedoodle before bringing one to join your home. This is where your breeder's expertise will be especially helpful. Reputable breeders can enlighten you as to any particular "quirks" the breed may possess, and what you can expect. They will also be available to you for the life of the dog, giving you the opportunity to keep them involved in your dog's development and life achievements. It is to your advantage to build a strong and healthy relationship with your Aussiedoodle breeder. It will benefit you, and it will also greatly benefit your puppy.

Basic Care of the Aussiedoodle

You are most likely already aware of the basic needs involved in caring for your Aussiedoodle puppy. You know you need to purchase high-quality food and to provide proper veterinary care, which includes scheduled vaccinations and flea and tick prevention. As a thoughtful owner, you've printed out the list of necessary supplies and purchased every last item on the list. But is there more to caring for an Aussiedoodle than you realize?

Aussiedoodle Puppies—What Do You Need to Know?

When it comes to an Aussiedoodle puppy, there really isn't much that sets the breed apart from other puppies of the same age when it comes to proper care. As with all puppies, your Aussiedoodle will require training to learn its place in your home and to grow up to be a well-mannered pooch. When training your puppy, basic socialization and puppy obedience classes can be helpful in establishing an easy to achieve criteria. Classes also provide you with a schedule which assists you in systematically teaching your dog new skills. But most of all, attending puppy classes exposes your puppy to new experiences in a positive environment. This type of exposure is extremely beneficial to your puppy's social development.

When training your Aussiedoodle puppy, consistency is the key to proper learning. All dogs do best when they understand their boundaries. You will want to establish now, that when you ask for a behavior, you expect to see it the first time you request it. Aussiedoodles are incredibly smart, and if you are not diligent in training your puppy, your puppy will soon train you!

Aussiedoodles are a breed that loves to please, and as such, they are exceptionally receptive to positive reinforcement training. Positive reinforcement training is a popular method that involves the use of treats and praise to train for the desired response in a dog. Its proponents assert that its techniques help to instill confidence and trust in your Aussiedoodle, as well as a love of training. This methodology strongly supports an attitude of rewarding good behavior with treats and praise and ignoring the bad. The theory is that over time, your dog will naturally repeat the behaviors that have been rewarded in the past and eliminate the ones that did not yield a treasure. A soft-natured breed, the Aussiedoodle could easily be crushed by aversive training methods. They are best avoided entirely, in favor of this purely positive approach to training.

How Much Exercise Should Your Aussiedoodle Puppy Get?

How much exercise a puppy should receive is the subject of great debate today. When it comes to an Aussiedoodle, the key principle you must always deal with is balance. Your Aussiedoodle will run all day long…if you let him. The problem is puppies have no concept of what is best for them, and your role as your dog's owner is to set healthy boundaries for your dog. As a dog breed with extremely high energy, it will be necessary for you to balance the amount of exercise that is healthy for your dog's age and development period, with its desire to be active. This is where engaging your dog's brain, as well as its body, is tremendously helpful.

Dogs become fatigued and physically and mentally satisfied through using both their bodies and their brains. A puppy who will grow to a medium-sized adult dog experiences a slower closing of the growth plates (the bones which will be properly joined together with cartilage and muscle upon maturity) than a smaller breed dog. With it taking approximately 18 months for an Aussiedoodle's growth plates to bond together, it is critical that your dog not engage in rigorous or lengthy activities, such as hiking or exceptionally long walks, prior to this age. To take part in these more strenuous activities at such a young age could have harmful effects on your dog's growth and development, and could lead to permanent or debilitating injury. Your dog was designed to do these things, but not until after 18 months of age. Your dog's body needs time to catch up with its drive.

For an Aussiedoodle puppy younger than 18 months of age, moderation is key. A moderate walk over level ground, which takes approximately half an hour a day is sufficient to meet the needs of your puppy. If you find your pup is bouncing off the walls and in need of a little more activity, take it for a second walk later in the day. For the health and safety of your puppy, it is best to increase the number of daily walks as opposed to the difficulty or length.

In addition to this, make use of puzzle toys, and even playtime with something like a tug toy to help tire out your puppy's brain. You will find when your pup's mind is tired, its body will also be.

Moderation and balance are always the governing principles when it comes to activity for your Aussiedoodle puppy. It is always best to err on the side of caution.

CHAPTER 8

Aussiedoodle Grooming— How Can You Make It Fun and Easy?

If an Aussiedoodle is to become a part of your life, you will need to spend time brushing your dog on a daily basis, to keep your dog's coat from developing painful mats. In addition to this, it will be important to locate a professional groomer to handle your dog's regular coat maintenance. Aussiedoodles require frequent grooming, both at home, as well as at a grooming shop. Though their coats may be low-shedding, equating to less cleaning for you at home, they are not low-maintenance. In fact, keeping an Aussiedoodle's coat in proper condition will take a big investment of both time and money. Grooming your Aussiedoodle is not optional, as failure to properly comb the hair on a nightly basis will lead to matting which can only be removed by shaving the coat. This process is very painful for your dog. If you are not prepared to brush your dog every night and to take your dog to the groomer every four to six weeks for maintenance grooming, you would be best to consider a breed with a lower-maintenance coat.

Aussiedoodles have high grooming requirements. You will need to commit to daily brushing and regular grooming appointments.

Aussiedoodle Grooming Basics

To be certain to start off on the right foot, you will want to get your Aussiedoodle puppy acquainted with being groomed from an especially early age. Your breeder most likely had your puppy on a table as young as five weeks old and began introducing it to grooming tools such as slicker brushes and combs. This early start is invaluable in getting your Aussiedoodle accustomed to what will become its daily grooming routine in a positive manner. Many breeders also like to make use of a dremel, a handheld sanding tool, to keep nails short. Using the dremel is begun during the puppy years, and is quite simple for an owner to maintain the process. If your breeder prefers this method for nail care, ask them to give you a demonstration, so you will have first-hand experience observing the process. After that, make one quick trip to the hardware store to purchase your dremel tool, and you're off to the races! Many breeders and dog owners prefer using a dremel to the more traditional guillotine style nail clippers as the chances of "nicking" your dog are slim to none, and you are able to get and keep the nails quite short. In addition to this, most dogs, once accustomed to the noise of the dremel, do not mind having their nails dremel-ed at all. Many will even fall asleep in your arms as you dremel away.

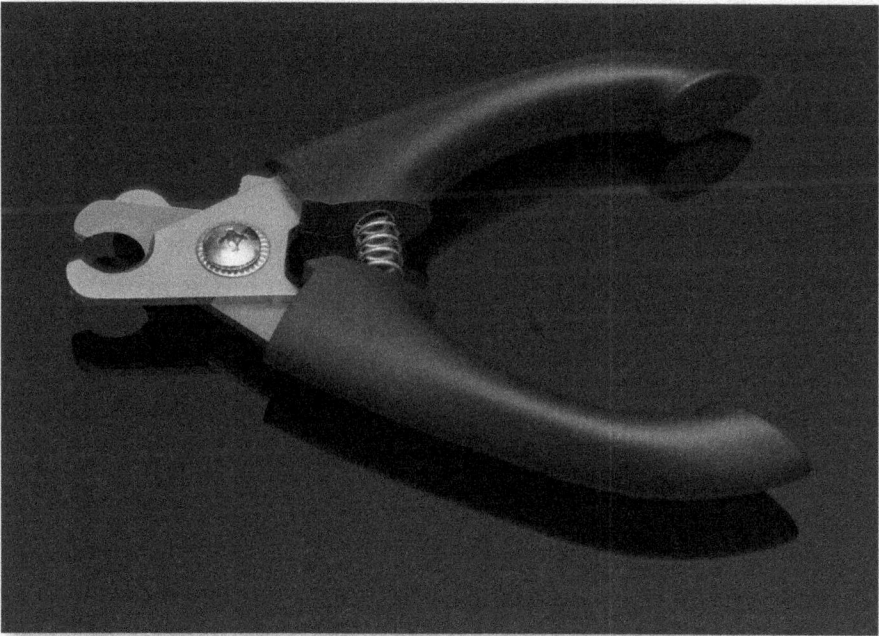

Guillotine style clippers are very popular.

If you plan to own an Aussiedoodle, you will need to be prepared to brush and comb your dog on a daily basis. Daily grooming is not optional with this breed. Failure to brush and comb your Aussiedoodle for several days could lead to a coat so matted and knotted, that it will be impossible to remove the tangles, meaning your dog must be completely shaved. Even missing a day or two can have disastrous consequences. If you own an Aussiedoodle, you will need to carve time out of your day, every day, to devote to coat maintenance.

But regular brushing at home is just the beginning of what your Aussiedoodle will require. If you prefer to keep your Aussiedoodle's fluffy coat, it will need to see a professional groomer once every four to six weeks, according to the rate of growth of your dog's coat. A professional groomer will properly bathe, condition, and blow dry your dog then provide any trim work that needs to be done to keep the dog's coat in excellent shape. Alternatively, you can have your groomer keep your Aussiedoodle's coat quite short. However, to maintain this style, your dog will still need to frequent the groomer's shop once every six to eight weeks. Regular combing and brushing at home are still recommended, even with a shaved dog.

Among other grooming services you or your groomer will need to provide are:

- **Regular ear cleaning**
  Ear cleaning is something that requires experience to do without causing injury to your dog. You can purchase an appropriate ear cleaning solution from your veterinarian.

While you are there picking up the cleaner, ask your veterinarian to demonstrate the proper way to clean your Aussiedoodle's ears. Since inserting anything in your dog's ears can potentially damage the eardrum, you must never insert any object, including cotton tips, in your dog's ears.

- **Tooth brushing or scaling**

Your veterinarian can also provide you with samples of toothpaste and a toothbrush to use to keep your Aussiedoodle's teeth sparkling clean. Your dog will not enjoy the process; however, it is an important part of regular dental care.

To get your Aussiedoodle used to teeth cleaning, it is best to approach toothbrushing a little bit at a time. Simply approach your dog with the toothbrush and gently brush a couple of teeth, taking care to clean the gums as well. If your dog tolerates this attention, lavishly praise it, and give it a treat. You can eventually work up to cleaning your dog's entire mouth.

Alternatively, you can buy a dental scaler from pet supply stores. Scalers allow you to work plaque away from the gum line, preventing any buildup of materials or bacteria that could lead to dental disease.

- **Nail care and maintenance**

Regular nail maintenance is important to keep your dog's feet healthy. Please see the above text for more information about nail care for your Aussiedoodle.

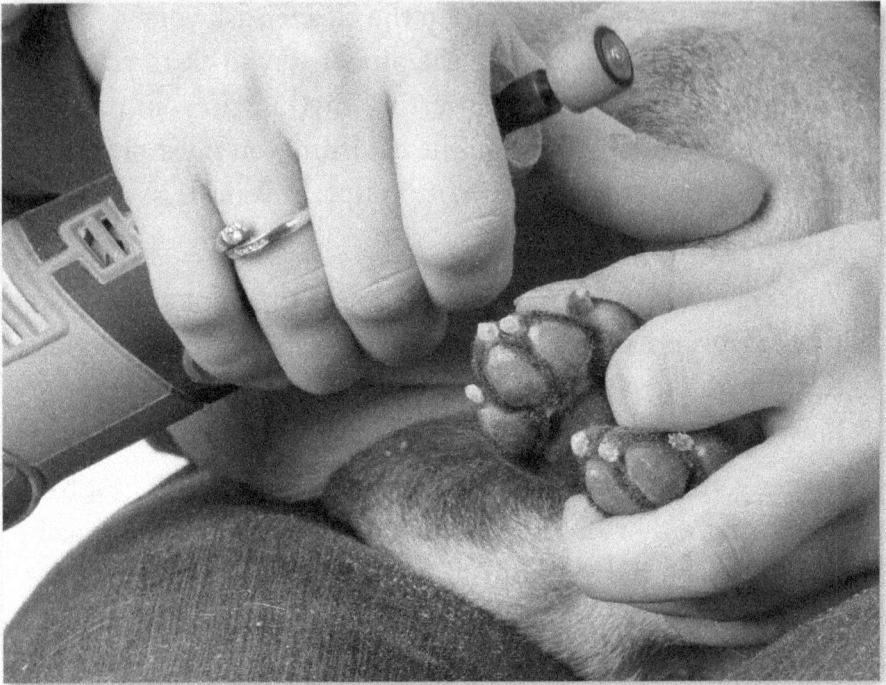

A dremel tool is a great way to keep
your Aussiedoodle's nails nice and short.

Aussiedoodle Dog Shampoos—Recommended Types

When it comes to Aussiedoodle shampoos, your groomer or your breeder will be able to provide more specific recommendations suited to your dog's unique needs. However, there are some basic guidelines you can follow to help you select the correct one.

Always use a shampoo that was formulated for dog use. Many different types of shampoos intended for human hair contain chemicals which are safe for use on humans, but that can have negative effects on dogs. In addition to this, human hair and dog hair are not the same, meaning they require different things from their shampoos in order for the hair to become clean and ripe for growth.

When selecting a dog shampoo, take time to read the label to find out what is in the product. If the product does not provide a list of ingredients, it is best to leave it on the shelf. Some pet shampoos contain products that will improve coat but at the possible expense of your dog's health. No product is worth that risk. The most toxic chemicals you should avoid include formaldehyde, sulfates, isopropyl alcohol, artificial colorings, and parabens.

Typically, products sold at department stores or pet suppliers are not of sufficient quality to properly care for your Aussiedoodle's coat. Your groomer can recommend the correct products to keep your dog's coat healthy, and they often sell them in their shops or will order them in for you.

Aussiedoodle Brushes—The Best Types for an Aussiedoodle's Coat

There are two tools you will need to keep your Aussiedoodle's coat in tip-top form: a slicker brush and a steel comb. A slicker brush is essentially a brush with a small rectangular head that is mounted sideways on the handle, meaning the longest part of the brush head runs parallel to the floor. The brush is equipped with small steel needle-like pins. They are quite delicate in nature and are a little sharp to the touch. Slickers are the perfect tool to neatly part through the Aussiedoodle coat, reducing tangles as it works. Many pet stores sell slicker brushes, and you can also order them online on many different grooming sites. They come in several different sizes. It is always a good idea to have both a medium and a large slicker for your Aussiedoodle. The medium is particularly helpful for working on your dog's feet.

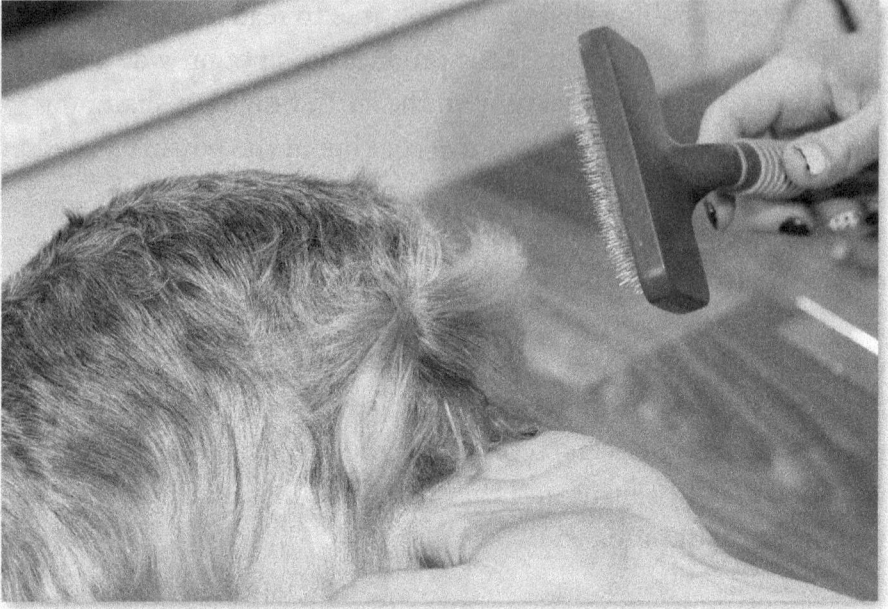

*A slicker brush is a necessary tool for keeping
your Aussiedoodle's coat tangle-free.*

A steel comb is also a necessary tool in the grooming arsenal of
any Aussiedoodle owner. This comb is a more precise tool for
gently removing any knots you might discover. Grooming combs
are also available in many different sizes and with varying tooth
designs. Choose a medium sized comb with moderately spaced
teeth for your grooming needs. A small one can also assist you
with delicately unraveling smaller tangles in the coat if need be.

Cleaning a Dirty Aussiedoodle

If your Aussiedoodle likes to dig in the mud or roll in something
a little more sinister, it is going to need a bath! Cleaning a
dirty Aussiedoodle is a challenging chore. If you bathe your
Aussiedoodle, you must also blow dry it. Otherwise, knots in the

coat will form, and they are very uncomfortable for your dog. For this reason, many owners simply take their dog to the groomer if they get very dirty. Alternatively, you can purchase a blow dryer, and bathe and blow dry your dog at home. If you opt to do this, you must be certain that you use your slicker brush to comb through the hair as you blow-dry, and you must get the coat completely dry. It is a long and tedious process that most owners, and their dogs, really prefer to leave to a professional groomer

Do Aussiedoodles Shed?

Aussiedoodles do shed. However, most shed very little. The product of two dogs known for their lower shedding properties, the ideal Aussiedoodle's coat is low to no-shedding; though as a hybrid, it is entirely possible that your puppy may favor its Australian Shepherd set of genes and have higher shedding properties than are preferable.

Are Aussiedoodles Hypoallergenic?

In truth, hypoallergenic dogs are a myth. Most people who are allergic to dogs are allergic to dander, not dog hair. Dander is essentially the pet equivalent of dandruff. It is dead skin cells which slough off the skin and become trapped on healthy skin or hair follicles. Dog hair often gets the blame, but it is dander that is the real culprit for allergy sufferers.

All dogs have dander. For that matter, so do all cats. However, dogs of a certain type of hair that is less likely to shed tend to trap more of the dander on their coats. Many believe that this trapping of hair leads to less of it in the air to induce allergic reactions.

Finding a Professional Groomer for Your Aussiedoodle

Finding a professional groomer that truly understands the Aussiedoodle's coat can be a challenge. One of the best resources available to you is your breeder. Your breeder has to have their dogs groomed somewhere, so they are likely to know someone in your area who is up to the task of regularly grooming your Aussiedoodle's coat.

Other Aussiedoodle owners may also have suggestions for you. Not sure where to find one? There are many different online groups on social media platforms that unite people who own the same breed. A quick search for Aussiedoodle groups might yield you with a treasure trove of information including the best techniques for brushing your dog as well as the name of the best groomer in town!

If all else fails, you can always conduct an internet search. Be sure to speak with the groomer ahead of time and ask all relevant questions to understand if the groomer is familiar with an Aussiedoodle's coat and is able to properly care for it. Some groomers will talk the talk but will be unable to walk the walk. Ask the groomer you are considering if they have a website where you can search for photos of dogs similar to yours, to see if their grooming style is what you are looking for.

CHAPTER 9

Aussiedoodle Training— Successfully Training Your Aussiedoodle

Training your Aussiedoodle can be so much fun! A breed that loves to work and lives to please, you will find your Aussiedoodle is eager to go wherever you do and to learn new lessons. However, Aussiedoodles can be stubborn, so you will need to be prepared to help your dog over any obstacles to learning that it might present. As a soft-natured breed, you will find your Aussiedoodle responds the best to positive reinforcement training techniques. One of the best things about this type of training is that you can do it anywhere. Just grab a clicker and some high-value treats, and you and your pooch are off to the races!

Aussiedoodles require some training. What could be better than playtime with a friend for a reward after a session?

What Tools Do You Need for Aussiedoodle Training?

There are very few tools required to train your Aussiedoodle, particularly if positive reinforcement training is the way you plan to go. Simply head out to your local pet store to pick up some high-value treats and a clicker, and you're ready to go!

What Treats Are Good for Positive Reinforcement Training for Your Aussiedoodle?

Choosing the right treats for training can be a challenge. Since you may need to give a large number of treats to teach then reinforce a new behavior or skill, you will want to choose something that is close to bite-sized and low in calories, while still big on flavor. Many owners like to make tuna fudge or liver cake. These recipes can be found on the internet and are easy to make in your own home, and can then be cut into small bite-sized pieces that are perfect for training. These types of treats are so pungent they may make your eyes water. But they will make your Aussiedoodle salivate and want to work for you, so they are worth your sacrifice, for sure!

Another great option for dogs who need to watch their weight is cat treats. Cat treats are bite-sized, crunchy, and typically very fragrant, making them the perfect choice for Aussiedoodle training sessions. You can purchase these at your local pet store, or even your veterinary clinic. Many vets use cat treats to distract a dog while they administer vaccinations because the treats are so effective at keeping a dog occupied.

You can also make use of leftover meats or cheese from your refrigerator cut into bite-sized pieces for training exercises.

Why is it necessary to use something high value? Dogs love treats, but over time, you will find that they are less willing to work for something that they receive on a regular basis. That's why you should stock your cupboards with lower value treats for everyday use, and high value treats that you pull out only for training sessions. It never hurts to have an added incentive on your side in the form of exceptionally tasty treats! Your Aussiedoodle will soon come to equate training time with something delicious to eat, and before long, training will be something that you both look forward to.

What Does Your Aussiedoodle Need to Learn?

There are several different skills every dog needs to learn in order to live life as an excellent canine member of society. But more than that, proper manners and basic obedience commands are tools that could potentially save your dog's life. It is very important to invest the time in training your Aussiedoodle to learn the most fundamental dog commands.

Positive reinforcement training is easy to do, and your dog will think it is lots of fun! To teach a dog any basic command, you only need two simple tools, a clicker, and some treats. As an example, we will use **"Sit"** as a stepping stone to learning. If you want your dog to **"sit,"** simply place a treat above your dog's head. For most dogs; when something is placed above their head, they will naturally sit. If your dog is reluctant to sit when the treat is placed over their head, you can either wait them out or simply assist them by gently moving their rear into the **"sit"** position. Once in place, you can click your clicker, showing your dog that it offered you the correct behavior, then immediately give your dog the treat. You can reinforce this behavior by repeating it several times since repetition is the key to learning! Once your dog seems to have mastered its command, you can continue to offer reinforcement by asking your dog to **"sit"** at random opportunities, and rewarding with a treat or praise for obedience to your request.

Dogs need to learn lots of skills to live happy and safe lives. Among the skills your dog needs to learn are:

- **"Sit"**

  "Sit" is one command that requires little training at all. In fact, for many dogs, **"sit"** is a default position. They automatically do it because it is comfortable for them. However, teaching your dog to sit on command can be an invaluable tool. There will be times in your Aussiedoodle's life where you will want them to take a seated position perhaps to wait to accept a treat or to proceed out the door for a walk. The **"sit"** command can be a precursor to more mannerly behavior and can be built upon to teach other commands more easily.

- **Down or flat**

  Teaching your dog to completely recline when asked to do so is also an important skill for your dog to have in its manners arsenal. Be consistent with whichever word you choose to "name" the behavior you are looking for. Consistency is the key to learning, so using **"flat"** and **"down"** interchangeably will confuse your Aussiedoodle, and set it up for failure and frustration. For some people, **"down"** is the command they want to use to ask a dog to remove themselves from someone or something. For others, it is the term they prefer when asking their dog to lie on something. Decide ahead of time, which is preferable to you and stick to it for best results.

- **Come**

  A reliable recall based on the command **"come"** is one of the most important skills your dog must learn. Of all obedience skills, this one is not optional as it could save your dog's life. The **"come"** command should be taught alongside **"stay,"** another invaluable life skill that could be critical to preventing accident, injury, or death for your dog. Always be certain that when your dog comes to you, it is an occasion for celebration! Ideally, you want your dog to come the first time you call, but you may have to work up to that level of reliability and "proof" the behavior in many different locales and under distraction before it will become something you can regularly count on. But whether your dog comes on attempt #1 or attempt #12, you never, ever want to scold a dog that comes to you. If you do, you will reinforce the idea that coming to you when called equates to you being upset with the dog for doing what it is told. You can work towards more dependability over time, but you must never show displeasure when your dog finally does obey and come to you when asked to do so, or it will have the opposite effect on your training efforts.

- **Off**

  Aussiedoodles need to learn to get off people and things when requested to do so. During the puppy years, this will be one of your most frequently repeated commands. Failure to remove themselves from an object or person when asked to do is very poor manners. Though it will take time, this is an important skill for your Aussiedoodle to master.

- **Leave it**

  Dogs love to get into things, and Aussiedoodles are especially good at finding things to put in their mouths that they ought not! Teaching the **"leave it"** command gives you a powerful tool to keep dogs from putting things in their mouths that could be very harmful to them. It is essentially the dog equivalent of teaching a child to not touch things unless given permission to do so.

- **Out**

  Sometimes we miss out on the opportunity for the **"leave it,"** and we must proceed straight to the **"out"** command. **"Out"** is simply a word to teach your dog that it must give you whatever it is that it had in its mouth or in its paws when requested to do so. This is another important skill that could save your dog's life. Be sure when you are teaching a dog to release an object to you that you always replace it with something better. In this way, the dog never becomes resentful of having to relinquish its "prize" because it knows if it gives something up, you are going to follow it up with an even better treasure!

- **Heel**

  Heeling is not just for obedience classes. There are times when you want your dog to focus on you exclusively, and your dog can't do that if it is six feet ahead of you, yanking on its leash with all its might. Teaching the heeling position is a foundation for good leash manners.

How Do You Deal with Unwanted Aussiedoodle Behaviors?

There will come a time when your Aussiedoodle displays behaviors that you really don't like. What is the best way to deal with such nuisance behaviors?

There are several approaches you can take to teaching your dog more appropriate behaviors, but the very first thing you must do is be patient. Rome wasn't built in a day, and you are not going to undo bad behavior in a day or two. It took time to establish the behavior, and it will take time to replace it with a better one.

Secondly, assess the situation to see what may be going on with your Aussiedoodle. Is your dog experiencing any changes in health, emotionally or physically, that could explain this sudden change? Has this behavior come on recently, or has it just reached the point where you can no longer tolerate it? How old is your dog? Is it possible your dog is going through a fear period or adolescent phase where training regression might occur? The answers to these questions can help you to determine what is really happening inside your Aussiedoodle's brain and best equip you to formulate the correct strategy for training the behavior you would like to see in your dog.

A great first step is often to go back to basics. It is entirely possible that your dog needs a refresher course. Be certain to never, ever reward the behavior you do not want to see; no matter how cute it might be. This is especially important when your Aussiedoodle is just a puppy. Dogs learn very quickly to repeat behavior they have seen reinforced in the past. This reinforcement could come in the way of a laugh or a smile; it does not have to be a food or toy reward. Cultivate a poker face for your training sessions with your pooch. It will be an invaluable tool for you.

Be consistent with training your Aussiedoodle. If you do not want to see a particular behavior from your dog, you must not allow it in any context; otherwise, you will confuse your dog and set back your training attempts.

As with all training for Aussiedoodles, this breed responds best to positive reinforcement training. In a breed so eager to please, harsh methods intended to correct will lead to a dog that is shut down and fearful and can ruin your bond with your dog. If you find that your attempts to teach better behavior using positive reinforcement techniques are not reaping any rewards, you most likely need to ask a professional behavior modification specialist to assist you. Always remember that not all professional trainers use the same methods, so you will need to carefully interview any behaviorists you contact to be sure their ideology and techniques are in line with how you want your dog to be treated and trained.

How Do You Properly Socialize Your Aussiedoodle?

Aussiedoodles are a breed that is known to be exceptionally friendly. Because of this, they will typically be quite amenable to any social activities you want to take them on! However, your Aussiedoodle will need to become familiar with its world, and since your home will be vastly different from their life at their breeder's house, it will be important for you to expose your dog to its new life and the adventures that entails. Even the most amiable dog can become shy, if not given the opportunity to approach new experiences with the support of their owner to instill confidence in their bravery.

The main things you will want to socialize your Aussiedoodle to are the following:

- **Other animals**
- **Adults**
- **Children**
- **Loud or unusual noises**
- **New environments**
- **Novel surfaces**

While most of this socialization will be started at your breeder's home, it is still important that you continue to provide these opportunities to your dog, especially up until the puppy reaches 16 weeks of age. Puppies learn the majority of all they will ever learn between the period of birth up to 16 weeks. They will continue to assimilate new skills after this point as well; however, those first 16 weeks are when puppies are most impressionable, and life experiences will form a lasting imprint on them. With this in mind, it cannot be overstated how important it is that a puppy's first experiences be only positive. Positive socialization opportunities leave a lifelong impact during this period, but so do negative ones, which can lead to fearfulness, shyness, and even aggression. You must be vigilant in protecting your puppy and setting it up to succeed. Never, ever allow your puppy to be in a situation that causes it discomfort, distress, and particularly, not pain. This can have a lifelong negative effect on your dog's emotional and social development.

With this in mind, it is vital that you always be aware of your Aussiedoodle's attitude towards the new thing you are exposing it to. If you want your dog to approach a stranger and it doesn't want to, do not force the dog to advance. This is the time to pay attention to what your dog is telling you. You can gently coax the dog in the direction you want it to go, rewarding with treats or praise for progress; but if a dog truly does not want to go, it is absolutely crucial that you do not force the issue. This is a time when you are building trust with your dog. By forcing a dog, you do not teach your dog that what it fears is not anything to be afraid of; you instead teach your dog that you are not trustworthy and don't have its best interests at heart.

To socialize to loud or unusual noises, many popular online video sites offer audio clips of different sounds such as airplanes taking off, babies crying, and the vacuum cleaner when in use. Play these sounds while your dog is going about its day in your home, and you will find your dog soon just accepts them as background noises that are no cause for attention or concern. This process is called desensitization and is very important to your dog's development.

Every dog will go through different fear periods. If you notice your puppy is suddenly very fearful of something that yesterday it thought was the greatest thing in the world, it is time to limit your puppy's exposure to new things, until this fearful time passes. It normally will only take a few days up to a week before you can proceed with socialization as a regular routine. Fear periods are times for retreating, not advancing.

Can You Train Your Aussiedoodle to Swim?

Aussiedoodles love to swim. With Poodle genes at work in their veins, there is no doubt that this breed enjoys the water. While you can teach your Aussiedoodle to swim in the water with you, it is often best to allow the dog to take the plunge into swimming entirely on its own. If your dog is going to be a water lover, you won't need to teach it to swim; it will just dive in and learn voluntarily! As with socialization, it is counterproductive to force your dog to do anything it doesn't want to do. Give your Aussiedoodle the space it needs to discover for itself if the water is the greatest thing since sliced bread, or not.

Is It a Good Idea to Train Your Aussiedoodle with a Shock Collar?

Aussiedoodles do not respond well to any type of training that is not reward or praise-based. For this reason, shock collar training is not a good idea for an Aussiedoodle. A dog with such an intense drive to please and of such high trainability is easy to motivate, meaning aversive tools such as shock collars are not necessary to achieve your desired results. But more than that, shock collars can damage your relationship with your Aussiedoodle and also change your dog's basic personality by inhibiting its natural jubilant and friendly attitude and replacing it with a fearful, neurotic, or worse, resentful dog. Shock collar training of an Aussiedoodle often leads to regression in previously learned behavior, and the development of new ways of coping, which are far less than desirable.

CHAPTER 10

Aussiedoodle Breeding— Getting Your Aussiedoodle Ready for a Litter

So, you think you might like to breed your Aussiedoodle? Breeding can be both exciting and frightening. If you are considering breeding your Aussiedoodle, there are many steps that you must take to ensure you and your dog are properly prepared. Breeding is not something that should be undertaken lightly. Not every dog should be bred. Though many myths persist that every dog should be permitted to have one litter to satisfy maternal instincts and settle temperament, nothing could be further from the truth.

If you want to breed your Aussiedoodle, it will be important to understand your motivations for doing so. Most reputable breeders do not make a profit on their litters, so if you had thought breeding would be a fun enterprise that might end up in a little financial gain, you would need to adjust your expectations. But in addition to this, our current world is experiencing a pet overpopulation problem. No matter how cute your dog is or how lovely you think their puppies might be, you do not want to contribute to the epidemic of homeless pets in America.

But more than all of this, it will be important to take some time to take stock of the dog you hope to use for breeding to understand what it is about him or her that you feel would be of value to future generations of the breed. Reputable breeders typically don't breed for money. They breed and show their dogs to help give back to a breed that they love. With many backyard breeders choosing to throw any two dogs together in the name of a buck, breeds can become diluted to the point they don't resemble their own standard anymore. But it is not just conformation and appearance that is compromised, indiscriminate breeding leads to health conditions in puppies, a heartbreak for the breed, the breeder, and the owners of those dogs.

Dogs who are to be bred should have some redeeming merits to contribute to the genetic pool. This becomes more complex when breeding mixed breed dogs such as the Aussiedoodle because, at present, there is no definitive standard. The breed is so young in its inception that there is a great deal of inconsistency that still exists in appearance, temperament, and personality. With this in mind, there are two things that you need to focus on: stringent health testing to ensure the two dogs you intend to mate are free from potential genetic disease and are in excellent health, and sound temperament.

As has been mentioned in a previous chapter, an aggressive dog should never be bred. Temperament can be shaped by a dog's environment; however, temperament is largely inherited. The two dogs you select for your breeding must display the most desirable traits of this hybrid which means you will want to breed together two dogs who are friendly, happy, intelligent, and affectionate by nature. These are hallmarks of the breed. Take care to avoid any extremes such as excessive hyperactivity, bouts of overexcitability, or neurotic behavior. Traits taken to excess in parents can often increase in intensity in puppies, so you want to be careful to avoid falling into this trap by choosing parents that display the ideal temperaments for both sides of the pedigree: the Australian Shepherd and the Poodle.

Since Aussiedoodles are intended to be companion dogs and cannot be shown in conformation shows due to their ineligibility for registration with standard kennel clubs, your puppies will be going to homes as pets only. This means that they will be loved and cherished family members, and temperament, though equally as important in a show dog, will be absolutely paramount. When you breed, you are making a commitment to stand behind your puppies and their owners for the life of the dog. If you produce dogs with temperaments that are not sound, you are sending liabilities out into the world. You are responsible for that, and it is something no breeder should take lightly. In addition to this, dogs with unstable temperaments often end up back at the breeder's home, or in a shelter or rescue. This is not ideal for the dog, and it is certainly not ideal for you or your puppy's owners. You can avoid all of this by only breeding dogs with exemplary temperaments. A passable temperament will not do. Only the best should ever be bred.

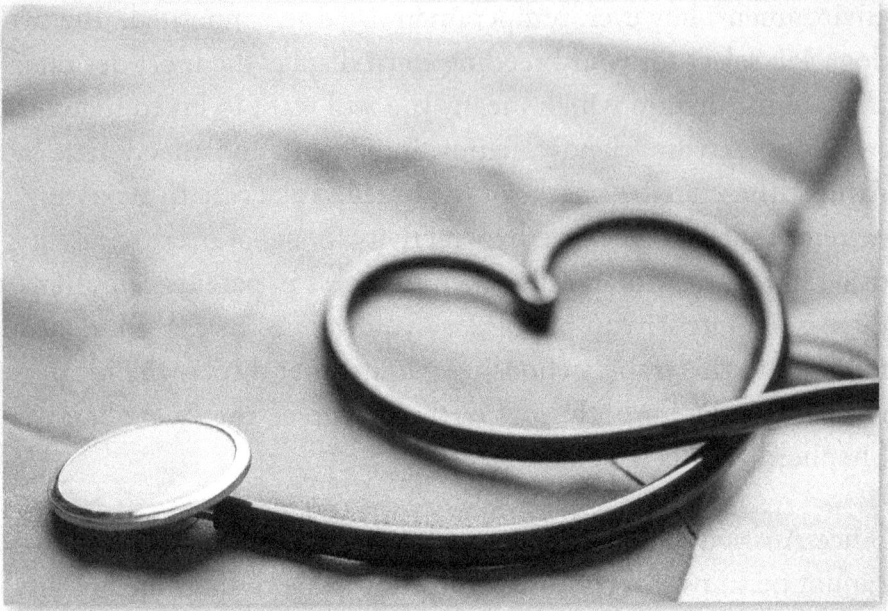

*Only Aussiedoodles who pass stringent health
testing specific to their heritage should be bred.*

Necessary Health Testing for Prospective Aussiedoodle Breeding Dogs

This brings us to the topic of health testing. When it comes to breeding, a standard wellness exam from your veterinarian is not sufficient to approve a dog for use in a breeding program. Since genetic illnesses and serious physical ailments can lurk beneath the surface of a dog, you will need to thoroughly screen both dogs for all possible genetic diseases and physical problems common to the breed. Should your dog not pass this rigorous screening; under no circumstances should the dog be bred.

The Poodle portion of your dog's pedigree may mean that your Aussiedoodle is prone to allergies. Though so much is yet unknown about allergies, it is believed there is a genetic component to it. If your dog suffers from allergies, this is yet another reason to rule out breeding that particular dog. Dealing with a lifelong allergy sufferer is frustrating for you and can be very painful for your puppy and your puppy's owners. You don't want to risk putting a family through that.

You can easily see that wanting your dog to experience a litter or to breed just because your dog is very cute is not a good idea. Breeding is a very serious responsibility. Many complications can arise during the breeding, whelping, and rearing process. They will cost you time, most of them will cost you money, and some will break your heart. It is not to be undertaken lightly. Bear in mind also, that it is possible that you could lose your bitch during the whelping process, leaving you grieving and with a litter of puppies who need your round the clock care to survive. You must carefully weigh the pros and cons before committing to breed your dog.

Here are the health tests every potential Aussiedoodle breeding dog should undergo and pass in order to be considered for use in a breeding program:

- **CAER testing to rule out Progressive Retinal Atrophy (PRA), Collie Eye Anomaly (CEA), and cataracts**

  CAER stands for Companion Animal Eye Registry. This type of test is required to certify that a dog's eyes are normal and permits results to be listed on the Orthopedic Foundation for Animals, a service which records health testing with the owner/breeder's permission for the public to view. All Aussiedoodle breeding dogs should be certified as having normal eyes to be considered for a breeding program.

The main eye issues that can befall an Aussiedoodle are Progressive Retinal Atrophy, Collie Eye Anomaly, and cataracts. The Aussiedoodle gets a double whammy of PRA genes as both the Australian Shepherd and the Poodle can be prone to developing this disease. Progressive Retinal Atrophy is defined as a progressive deterioration of the retina. The disease is painful and eventually leads to blindness.

Collie Eye Anomaly is a hereditary defect affecting the integrity of the dog's eye. The condition can be minor or quite serious and can lead to vision impairment and even blindness.

Cataracts typically emerge shortly after birth or prior to a dog reaching three years of age. Cataracts in dogs most often do lead to blindness.

- **Echocardiogram to rule out Mitral Valve Disease**

  Mitral Valve Disease is common to both Australian Shepherds and Poodles, which makes it also common to the Aussiedoodle. Mitral Valve Disease, which is essentially an enlarging of the heart muscle causing heart murmurs, breathing difficulties, and possible fluid on the lungs, can be detected on an x-ray. Should Mitral Valve Disease be suspected, an echocardiogram is necessary to determine the extent of the illness in the dog. Any dog who presents with a heart issue is unsuitable for breeding.

- **OFA or PennHip testing for Hip and Elbow Dysplasia**

  If the femur joint of a dog does not rest properly in the hip socket, hip and elbow dysplasia is the result. Hips and elbows can be affected by nutrition and environmental factors, but the largest determining factor is the hip and elbow scores of a dog's parents. Both OFA and PennHip bestow "grades" or "scores" which reveal the extent of a dog's hip and elbow condition. These grades can range from a fail to fair, normal, good, and even excellent. You want to give great consideration to breeding a dog with only fair hips and elbows, and if you opted to do so, the dog should be bred only to other Aussiedoodles with good or excellent scores to improve the chances of producing good or excellent hips and elbows. Normal, good, or excellent grades are acceptable in Aussiedoodle breeding stock.

- **OFA Patella exam to test for Luxating Patellas**

  Luxating Patellas is another condition which is common to both the Australian Shepherd and the Poodle. A luxating patella is essentially knee cap that slips out of place. This condition is incredibly painful and can lead to excruciating tears of ligaments and tendons, which would require extensive surgeries to repair.

  The test for luxating patellas is quite simple and can be conducted by your veterinarian in his or her office. As with hips and elbows, patellas are given grades, but their scale is numeric. Only dogs with patellas that cannot be luxated are suitable for breeding.

- **Blood work to screen for Hypothyroidism and Pelger Huet Anomaly**

  An improperly functioning thyroid produces too little hormone. Hypothyroidism is genetic. Common symptoms include weight gain, excessive hunger, lethargy, and poor coat texture.

  Pelger Huet Anomaly is a very rare genetic condition; however, all breeding dogs should be tested for the gene as it can cause jaw and skeleton deformities and issues with proper cartilage growth and development.

- ## DNA testing for Von Willebrand's Disease

  DNA tests are quite simple. You order a set of swabs from a lab, take the swabs to the vet who then takes a sterile sample from your dog, and off the swabs go for processing. In several weeks, your lab of choice will contact you with the results.

  Von Willebrand's Disease is a condition of the blood where a dog lacks the ability for its blood to clot properly.

These tests provide a baseline standard from which you can determine if your dog is healthy enough to be bred. If your dog receives a failing score in even one of these areas; for the health and safety of the next generation, the dog should be eliminated as a breeding option. This does not mean your dog will befall the condition themselves. In many cases, it simply means they have the ability and likelihood to reproduce it in offspring, and as such, the responsible thing to do is to spay or neuter the dog and allow them to enjoy life as a beloved family pet.

The Female Aussiedoodle–Getting Ready for Breeding

If you own a female Aussiedoodle who has passed all required health screening, you will want to begin getting her ready for breeding when she has passed her second birthday. Though some people opt to breed younger, a female Aussiedoodle is still very much a puppy herself until two years of age, and it is important to allow her to fully mature before she becomes a mother.

You can begin health testing after your girl is a year old; however, some tests such as hips, elbows, and patellas are age specific. You will need to refer to your veterinarian or the OFA website to find what ages a dog must be in order to qualify for testing.

Timing is critical when it comes to breeding. Females generally cycle one to two times yearly. Though pregnancy can occur at any time during a heat, girls are most typically fertile between the 7th to 10th days of the 30-day cycle. The only accurate way to determine if a girl is ovulating and ready for mating is to progesterone test daily, starting around Day 7. However, once a female dog will willingly stand for a male, she is most often ready to be bred. When a female has entered the most fertile period of her cycle, it is important that you breed her to the male every other day until she will no longer allow him to mount her. This gives you the best chance at successful breeding.

Most often the female dog is taken to the home of the stud dog for this service to be performed. If a great distance is involved, the female is often sent alone via plane and returned once the breeding has been accomplished.

Prior to mating, it is important to continue excellent care of your girl. Feed her high quality, nutritious food, and supplements to keep her healthy and strong.

The Male Aussiedoodle—Getting Ready for Breeding

The stud dog should always be fed high-quality, nutritious food as well. Of primary concern with the stud dog is keeping his sperm in excellent condition. If indeed, a dog has passed all of his health testings and is of sufficient quality to be used to sire puppies, it will be necessary to periodically take your dog to the vet to have him "collected." Collecting your dog essentially cleans his system of old sperm to allow him to replenish it with a new, more vital supply. Prior to breeding, it is always a good idea to collect and evaluate a dog's semen to ensure that it is still excellent quality and has the ability to produce puppies.

Care must be taken to ensure the temperature in your home is amenable to brewing strong, virile sperm. Moderate temperatures are best. During the summer months, keeping your house cool will help with any potential reproductive attempts.

Sourcing a Good Quality Aussiedoodle Stud Dog

During the year prior to breeding, you will need to select a suitable mate for your female Aussiedoodle. This process requires very careful consideration. You will want to acquaint yourself with pedigrees from all of the available Aussiedoodle stud dogs to understand what the lineage is behind each of the males you see today. You will also need to carefully assess your female to understand her strengths and what her weaknesses are. This will assist you in determining what you hope to improve on in breeding your female.

In selecting the ideal male for your female, you will want to consider ones who have the qualities your female lacks and that you hope to see reproduced in the offspring. Bear in mind that no dog is perfect but glaring "faults," and particularly failed health clearances, are a clear no-no.

Once you have discovered the male you feel is best suited to your female, you will then need to approach the owner to discuss their willingness to allow you to use their male for stud. A fee is associated with this which is typically equivalent to the cost of a puppy. In some cases, a breeder would prefer to take the "pick" or best puppy from the litter, in lieu of a stud fee. These are all negotiable factors you and the stud owner can discuss.

A stud fee can be paid out at the time of the breeding, by deposit with the balance due when the puppies are born, or when the puppies go to their new homes. Typically, a contract is signed prior to breeding. The contract will clearly outline what is expected of each party, and your signatures make it a legally binding contract between the two of you. Standard stud contracts specify what "constitutes" a breeding, and what happens should pregnancy not occur. For most stud owners, successful breeding is defined as two live puppies at birth. If fewer than two are born than that, the owner of the female is often entitled to what is called a "return service" or a second breeding attempt, at no charge. If the dam fails to "take," a return service is also often offered in the standard agreement.

Newborn Aussiedoodle Puppies—Their Care and Feeding

Newborn Aussiedoodle puppies require very little care from their breeder. Their mother will attend to their cleaning and feeding. Your primary role is to record weights and monitor the mother dog to ensure all of her needs are being met. She will need excellent quality nutrition to ensure enough milk supply to feed her hungry brood. Once the puppy's eyes open around Day 12, and the puppies begin to urinate and defecate on their own, the breeder's job begins. You will then have the responsibility of frequently cleaning up bowel movements and pee spills, to prevent puppies from inadvertently rolling in their own mess. When the puppies begin to develop sharp little teeth, you will then need to transition them from drinking their mother's milk exclusively, to a mush, which will eventually be replaced by kibble, prior to leaving the nest at eight weeks of age.

Having puppies in the house is a busy time for a breeder and for the mother dog. There is much critical socialization to be done, cleaning and puppy pen maintenance, and just enjoying your puppies. They are such a treasure and are with you for such a short amount of time that you really need to spend as every opportunity with them that you can. They grow up way too fast!

Aussiedoodle puppies love to socialize!

CHAPTER 11

Aussiedoodle Lifestyle— What is it Like to Live with an Aussiedoodle?

There is no doubt that there will be a bit of an adjustment period when learning to live with an Aussiedoodle. Aussiedoodles are known to bring much joy to their families. You will wonder how you ever got along without one! However, it is always a good idea to understand what to expect when you bring an Aussiedoodle to join your home.

Life with an Aussiedoodle is always lots of fun!

Becoming a Savvy Aussiedoodle Owner

Understanding your Aussiedoodle is key to establishing a great relationship with your dog. Your Aussiedoodle is a highly intelligent dog with energy to spare. As such, if you are not currently an active person, it's time to buy a good pair of running shoes because your Aussiedoodle is going to help you get in better shape! This intense energy level comes as a surprise to some families. Though hybrids can be inconsistent in temperament, even the most laidback Aussiedoodle is still going to require a significant amount of time when it comes to expending natural energy.

Getting Your House Ready for Your Aussiedoodle Puppy

As with any puppy, you will need to "puppy proof" your house prior to bringing your Aussiedoodle to join your home. To do this, it is important to take a look around to pinpoint things that could be hazardous to your Aussiedoodle. Remember that puppies are mischievous opportunists on the hunt for something to play with or chew! You will want to remove any items from the floor that your Aussiedoodle could get into that you either don't want to be destroyed or that could lead to harm for your dog. This includes placing shoes behind closet doors, and ensuring all electrical cords are unplugged and placed out of reach.

You will then need to decide where to place water and food bowls for easy access as well as dog beds. Ideally, you want access to food and water to be in a central location that is both easy for you to prepare the meal and convenient for your dog to access it and its water when needed. Dog beds can be distributed throughout the highest traffic areas of your home. After all, your Aussiedoodle is going to want to be wherever the action is, and that is where you are!

Other items you will need to pick up include toys, a collar, and a leash. Buy a random sampling of toys. Over time, your Aussiedoodle will show a preference for a particular style, and you will have a better idea of what types of things your Aussiedoodle prefers, so you will know what to stock up on.

You will also need to decide ahead of time where your Aussiedoodle will sleep. Some owners like their dogs to sleep with them while others prefer their dogs to rest in a crate or a dog bed either beside their bed or in another room in the house.

You will need to get your dog's sleeping area set up, so you can introduce your Aussiedoodle to it as soon as you bring it home for the first time.

Are Cages a Good Idea for an Aussiedoodle?

Cages, which are also known as crates or kennels, can be an excellent tool for your Aussiedoodle. If approached properly and used as a place of refuge and not one of punishment, your Aussiedoodle may soon come to see its cage as a place to retreat for a little rest or to play with a toy. Cages are also an excellent tool for assisting with house training. But more than all of this, there are times when your dog will need to be in a cage for their own safety and protection. Some of these situations include a trip in your vehicle, at dog sports events, or even when visiting the vet and requiring extended care. For this reason, it is an excellent idea to introduce your Aussiedoodle to a crate and teach your dog that it is an awesome place to be! Wonderful DVDs and online videos exist teaching you a variety of different crate games that can help your dog to learn that crates can be fun.

Additionally, you will need a place for your dog to go when you cannot be home to supervise them. A cage provides the perfect solution to that and is all the more reason that teaching your dog that their cage is a haven and not prison is a wonderful idea!

If your dog needs to spend an extended amount of time in a crate or cage, you will want to be sure to give it something to do in there. Rubber toys with openings that can be stuffed with tasty things, raw meaty bones, or even a favorite toy will keep your dog quite content until you return home to let it out.

Do You Need a Kennel for an Aussiedoodle?

Outdoor kennels can be a great solution for dogs who love being outdoors and need more room to roam. However, Aussiedoodles are dogs that thrive when in the company of their owners. An outdoor kennel run can be useful for when you are outdoors working in your yard, and your dog wants to tag along. They are an especially good idea if you don't have a fenced in backyard or if your Aussiedoodle has proven to be a fence jumper, and you need something a little more secure.

It is never recommended that you leave an Aussiedoodle in an outdoor run unsupervised, or for any length of time. Since these dogs exist to be sociable, an Aussiedoodle left to their own devices in a kennel run can become obsessive, neurotic, destructive, and even depressed.

Aussiedoodles and Dog Doors—Do You Need a Dog Door in Your Home?

Installing a dog door in your home is a relatively simple thing to do. It can also save you untold hours letting your Aussiedoodle in and out whenever the mood strikes it. However, while a dog door can seem like the perfect solution, it will only be a good tool for you if your Aussiedoodle thinks staying in its own backyard is an excellent idea. If your dog has proven trustworthy, free access to your backyard when you are home might be just what the doctor ordered. However, if your dog has a penchant for jumping or climbing fences, this will not be a good idea for your particular dog.

If you do opt to add a dog door to your home, be certain you have the ability to close it off when necessary, barring your Aussiedoodle access to your backyard, from time to time. If you cannot be home to supervise or check on your Aussiedoodle's outdoor time, it is best to cordon off the yard. With the rise of unsavory characters entering homeowner's property unawares as well as owning a highly intelligent breed capable of contriving an escape from even the most secure containment system, you never want to leave your Aussiedoodle with free rein of your yard when you are not on the premises.

Aussiedoodles and Dog Gates—Do You Need to Install a Dog Gate?

Dog gates, also known as baby gates, are an excellent way to keep your Aussiedoodle contained to specific areas of the house. These can be especially effective if you are trying to clean, and your Aussiedoodle's insistence on "helping" would derail the entire process. Bear in mind that most Aussiedoodles can climb, jump, or even knock down baby gates, so they aren't one hundred percent foolproof. However, they are an inexpensive solution that will buy you some free time to get things done in other areas of the house, without Aussiedoodle interference.

Should You Allow Your Aussiedoodle on Your Furniture?

Whether or not you allow your Aussiedoodle on your furniture is a matter of personal preference. What is important is that your Aussiedoodle understands its place. This does not mean that you have to banish your dog to only spending its time on the floor. You can teach your Aussiedoodle that it is permitted on your furniture when invited to join you there, but it must relinquish its position when asked to leave. In this way, your dog understands that being on the furniture is a privilege and not a right.

CHAPTER 12

Aussiedoodle Health— What Do You Need to Know?

Though Aussiedoodles can suffer from a number of health ailments and conditions, they are typically quite a healthy breed. The Australian Shepherd and the Poodle both enjoy excellent longevity, and they have passed these wonderful traits along to their Aussiedoodle offspring. However, both the Australian Shepherd and the Poodle do have certain genetic predispositions towards certain physical diseases. If you have chosen your breeder very carefully, your Aussiedoodle's parents should have been carefully health tested prior to being approved for breeding, giving you the assurance that your puppy is not at risk for genetic disease. However, some health condition, such as patella issues can develop later in life. It is always a good idea to understand what common ailments can affect your breed to help to know what to be on the lookout for.

What are Common Aussiedoodle Health Problems?

Aussiedoodles have a fairly short list of problems that can befall the breed. Discussed more in-depth in the chapter on breeding and necessary health testing, here is a list of known genetic diseases and physical problems which can befall an Aussiedoodle:

- Eyes—Progressive Retinal Atrophy, Collie Eye Anomaly, Cataracts
- Hip and Elbow Dysplasia
- Hearts—Mitral Valve Disease
- Luxating Patellas
- Endocrine Disorders--Hypothyroidism, Cushing's Disease

  These diseases affect the normal functioning and release of the thyroid hormone. If your dog presents with any of the symptoms of either disease which can include hair loss, weight gain, and excessive lethargy, there is no cure. However, synthetic hormone therapy can help alleviate side effects and allow your dog to live a normal, happy life.

- Pelger Huet Anomaly

  Pelger Huet Anomaly is an extremely rare genetic disorder which affects the proper development of the skeletal and musculature systems. There is no known treatment for this disease.

- Von Willebrand's Disease

  Von Willebrand's Disease is present when a dog lacks the correct enzyme for their blood to clot properly. There is no treatment for this disease; however, should your dog have an accident where there is a lot of blood loss incurred, a blood transfusion may be necessary.

  As Hypothyroidism, Cushings Disease, Pelger Huet Anomaly, and Von Willebrand's Disease are all genetic disorders; unfortunately, there is nothing that can be done to minimize the risks of developing them. The only course of action to prevent future generations from befalling these illnesses is to only breed dogs who that have been DNA tested and received "clear" health results for each of the aforementioned disorders.

Aussiedoodles and Bloat—Is Bloat a Problem for the Aussiedoodle?

Though Bloat, also known as Gastric Dilatation Volvulus, is more typically a problem for large breed dogs, it can also pose a problem for Aussiedoodles. Unfortunately, to date, it is not known what causes Bloat, but it is most commonly fatal.

Bloat is what occurs when fluid, food, or gas builds up around the stomach and causes the abdomen to inflate. This inflation increases pressure on vital organs, which can lead to breathing obstructions, restricted blood flow to the heart and brain, or a rupture in the stomach. Bloat can lead to a condition known as torsion, where the dog's intestines twist. This is a very painful ailment, which most often results in death.

It is believed Bloat may be caused by the following factors:

- Eating only one large meal per day
- Consuming food or water for a raised dish
- Eating too quickly
- Rigorous activity directly after eating
- Genetic predisposition
- Anxiety

Bloat most commonly affects breeds who are large in size and who possess deep chests. Though this does not describe your average Aussiedoodle, Aussiedoodles are guilty of many of the aforementioned behaviors, including eating too quickly, exercising directly after a meal, and genetic predisposition.

What Vaccinations Will Your Aussiedoodle Need?

All dogs require vaccinations, and your breeder and your vet can best advise what your Aussiedoodle puppy needs. Typically, at age eight weeks and just prior to your puppy joining your family, your puppy should receive its first shot in a three-shot series which is then boostered at age one year. This series of vaccinations piggyback on any remaining maternal antibodies your puppy will have from consuming its mother milk and will reinforce and support the antibodies already at work in your puppy's body. This three vaccination series of shots should include the following immunizations:

- Distemper
- Adenovirus
- Parvovirus
- Parainfluenza

This initial series of shots is known as DA2PP and is commonly referred to as a puppy's core vaccines. These shots are most commonly administered several weeks apart with the most typical schedule being at 8 weeks, 12, and finally 16. The DA2PP vaccine should be boostered at age one for maximum efficacy. Many veterinarians claim this series of shots is effective for three years; however, much evidence supports that vaccinating again so soon is unnecessary and poses health risks for your puppy. As an alternative, speak to your veterinarian about a routine blood test called a titer. Titering tests for remaining antibodies in your dog's body from its initial set of core vaccines. Should sufficient antibodies linger in your dog's system, it is unnecessary to vaccinate the dog again.

Your dog should also receive a Rabies shot at six months of age or later if possible. Though many veterinarians do recommend boostering the Rabies shot at one year of age, leading vaccination experts say this is unnecessary. If you are uncertain about what is best for your Aussiedoodle, you can always schedule an appointment to discuss proper vaccination options with your veterinarian.

Should You Give Your Aussiedoodle Vitamins?

Though vitamins are essential to your Aussiedoodle's growth and development, supplementing your dog's vitamin supply on your own is not advised. Your veterinarian is your best resource for understanding what your dog may be lacking and how best to remedy the problem. The food you feed your Aussiedoodle should be sufficiently fortified to meet all of your dog's nutritional requirements, which includes daily minerals and vitamins.

Keeping Your Aussiedoodle at a Healthy Weight

Keeping your Aussiedoodle's weight healthy requires a balanced approach. The first step to achieving this is regular, daily exercise. Most owners never have to worry about their Aussiedoodle becoming overweight or obese because of the breed's natural desire to be as active as possible. Regular exercise is an important component to physical health and body condition, but in an

Aussiedoodle, it is also necessary for mental well-being. An Aussiedoodle who does not receive regular daily exercise will not be a happy dog.

The amount and type of food you feed will also significantly impact the condition of your Aussiedoodle. Feeding poor quality food full of fillers is more likely to add unnecessary pounds on your Aussiedoodle's frame. This puts excess strain on your dog's skeletal system, which can increase the likelihood of developing hip, knee, or elbow problems.

But the amount of food you feed is equally as important to the type. It is never recommended that you allow your Aussiedoodle to free feed. Leaving a dish of dog food out for your dog to eat whenever it feels like it is a recipe for gaining weight. It is best to control the portion you give to your dog to maintain appropriate weight levels. To understand how much food your dog should be getting daily, read the recommended amounts on the side of the bag. This will differ a bit according to your dog's activity level. Dogs who are excessively active will require more daily food than those who only receive a moderate level of activity. Your vet can best help you customize the amount that is correct for your Aussiedoodle.

What is a Healthy Amount of Food for an Aussiedoodle?

Experts recommend feeding your Aussiedoodle between two to three cups of food per day. Your dog should receive a higher amount if very active and the lower amount if only moderately active. You can adjust the amounts accordingly as you observe your dog's physical condition. Should your dog appear overly thin, you may want to increase portions slightly, and reduce them if your dog seems to be getting portly.

Always bear in mind if you are doing a lot of training and feeding extra treats, you may also need to make adjustments to meal portion

CHAPTER 13

Aussiedoodles— The Golden Years

Into each life some rain must fall, and sadly, our Aussiedoodles will get old. Caring for a dog in their senior years requires specialized care. Though an extremely hardy breed, you will notice your Aussiedoodle slowing down with age. This change in energy doesn't mean that your dog no longer wants to go for walks. It simply means that activity levels need to be adjusted to reflect what is appropriate for your dog's age and health condition. With excellent care, your Aussiedoodle's senior years truly can be golden!

Aussiedoodle Changes in the Golden Years

Though it is impossible to predict the precise age your dog will become a geriatric, most veterinarians define the senior years as beginning at age eight. You will notice your Aussiedoodle undergoing a number of different physiological and behavioral changes as it ages. It always helps to have an idea of what you can expect, so you are not taken by surprise by what may seem like an unusual activity for your dog.

Aussiedoodle Physiological Changes

Aussiedoodles experience similar physical changes to what aging humans undergo. Some of the most common problems your dog may struggle with include arthritis, hearing loss, stiff joints, reduced bladder capacity, and pain.

Aussiedoodle Behavioral Changes

Most behavioral changes owners see in their Aussiedoodles are the result of a dulling of the senses. Eyes and ears don't work as well as they once did, and even your Aussiedoodle's memory may become quite foggy. You may find that your Aussiedoodle now startles to once familiar sounds and is not quite as jovial as it used to be. This change in personality is often attributed to aching joints and bones that creak and moan when your dog tries to rise from its bed or attempts to engage in regular exercise.

Aussiedoodle Health–Caring for Your Geriatric Aussiedoodle

An aging Aussiedoodle requires a different type of care to a dog in its prime. In order to help your older Aussiedoodle remain comfortable, here are some things that you should endeavor to do:

- **Make regular visits to your veterinarian.**

  Wellness checks are very important in keeping your senior Aussiedoodle comfortable and healthy. It is recommended that you visit your veterinarian every six months. This will allow your vet the opportunity to monitor your dog's health and make a note of any decline in physical or emotional health. Regular veterinary care is key to detecting any sign of pain, illness, or disease, and can buy your Aussiedoodle more quality time with you.

- **Avoid rough play.**

Just because your Aussiedoodle is old doesn't mean it won't still want to play! Though your dog's body is elderly, its brain is still quite young. This means that sometimes your geriatric Aussiedoodle will roughhouse now and pay for it later. To ensure your dog does not do itself any harm, limit play time to specific time increments and always supervise any play carefully. If you have puppies or overexuberant dogs in the house, it may be best to limit their time with your elderly Aussiedoodle to reduce the risk of injury or pain.

- **Limit exercise.**

Though your Aussiedoodle may be convinced it is still young, it isn't. For this reason, adjustments to your dog's regular exercise routine must be made. Decrease the duration and the difficulty of walks; always aiming for moderation.

- **Change to a senior-friendly food.**

Your Aussiedoodle's lifestyle will change in the senior years, and as such, it will no longer need a food that is so high in protein or calories. To avoid weight gain and strain on the kidneys and liver, it is best to switch your Aussiedoodle's food to something comprised of a lean protein source. As always, continue to purchase the highest quality food that you can afford.

- **Provide access to clean drinking water.**

You may find your Aussiedoodle is thirstier than ever! This could be due to reduced kidney capacity. Keeping your dog well-hydrated is key to maintaining health in the senior years. Always ensure that your dog's water dish is full of clean water.

- **Consider warmth.**

  Aging Aussiedoodles feel the cold more than their younger counterparts. This is the perfect time to consider purchasing a heated bed or even just to make use of a heating pad where your Aussiedoodle can cuddle up and stay cozy.

- **Provide help with stairs**

  At some point, you will find your Aussiedoodle can no longer safely navigate stairs. If your home has a number of areas with stairs in them, you may want to make a central area of your house that is near to the outside the gathering place for the whole family. If your dog needs to go up and down stairs, carrying your Aussiedoodle may be your best option.

- **Make the most of your time**

  Sadly, your Aussiedoodle will not live forever. Every moment is precious. With this in mind, make your dog's senior years the best of its life by taking every opportunity for cuddles, kisses, treats, and fun. Your senior Aussiedoodle will be most content when you are near.

Aussiedoodle Endings—Saying Goodbye to Your Senior Aussiedoodle

Saying goodbye to your Aussiedoodle is a very difficult thing. Most veterinarians ask owners to assess if their dog is having more good days than bad in making the decision. The truth we must always bear in mind is that our dogs are masters at hiding their pain, and they will often linger on simply because our hearts aren't ready to let them go.

Only you can decide when it is time for your Aussiedoodle to pass from this life to the next. It is a decision that is not to be taken lightly. But in general; when your dog no longer is able to enjoy the things in its life that it always cherished, it is likely time to let go. Your veterinarian can assist you with this decision.

There is always a grieving process after saying goodbye to your Aussiedoodle. Grieving is unique to each person, but it is important to allow yourself to express the depth of your loss in order to heal. Some people feel the best way to honor the memory of a beloved pet is to get a puppy or adopt a rescue Aussiedoodle. For them, it may be the perfect solution. But you may feel very differently when your time comes, and that is okay. As you grieve the loss of your most faithful friend, be patient with yourself, and take all the time you need. Those who love deeply also hurt deeply when their beloved dog passes on. This is a fitting tribute to a cherished Aussiedoodle friend.

CHAPTER 14

Conclusion

I f you are looking for the ideal family companion to keep you active and ready for adventure, you won't be disappointed with an Aussiedoodle. Full of energy, affection, and fun, the Aussiedoodle is the perfect addition to family living, especially if kids are a part of the package. A breed with a relatively short history, there is no doubt that the Aussiedoodle is here to stay.

Owning an Aussiedoodle will change your life...for the better.

A breed with a rich heritage as a working dog, the Aussiedoodle excels at hunting, retrieving, scent work, agility, dog performance sports, herding, and more. In fact, for an all-around athletic dog with the drive and stamina to succeed, you can't beat an Aussiedoodle! Today, their primary function is as a beloved family companion, a job at which the breed excels. But as an avid sportsman, the Aussiedoodle is the contender to beat in many sports including agility, flyball, Rally-O, and competitive obedience. Known affectionately as both a canine "Einstein" and a "Velcro Dog," the Aussiedoodle is incredibly intelligent, friendly, loyal, and loving both to its family and strangers.

If an Aussiedoodle is in your future, be sure to do your research very thoroughly and only purchase a dog from a reputable breeder. Avoid backyard breeders, pet stores, puppy mills, and online marketplaces, which can lead you astray. A reputable breeder will stringently health test their breeding stock and provide you with written health guarantees to ensure your puppy is free from any potential hereditary illness. Understand ahead of time what questions you should ask your prospective breeder to be certain they are a breeder of character and integrity that you can trust. Know the pitfalls to avoid and take every precaution to steer clear of them.

Aussiedoodles enjoy great longevity with life expectancies ranging from ten to thirteen years. A breed with few serious potential health concerns, you will need to be aware that hips, elbows, eyes, patellas, thyroid, and heart problems can befall the breed. This is why it is exceptionally important that you see proper health clearances for any genetic conditions which the parents could carry. Normal health ratings will give you peace of mind that all due diligence has been done to produce a healthy puppy that will bring your family joy for a decade or more.

Though Aussiedoodles do not require any higher financial investment than any other breed, you will still need to supply the best food and veterinary care possible to keep your Aussiedoodle healthy and strong. You will also need to purchase some everyday supplies such as a leash, collar, bed, toys, a crate, and training treats and tools. Be sure to bring your Aussiedoodle along when you shop to help you select the correct sizes for important items such as collars, leashes, and cages.

Choosing to add an Aussiedoodle to your home is a serious commitment. You will need to be sure that you are ready for the added responsibility of caring for a breed with high energy requirements. A thorough understanding of the breed will help you in your quest for a well-mannered pooch that you can proudly take anywhere. But your hard work and effort will be well worth it for when you add an Aussiedoodle to your home, you will wonder how life could get any better. It probably can't... unless you buy another! Enjoy your journey as the proud owner of a beautiful Aussiedoodle.

Your Comprehensive Aussiedoodle Resource List

Primarily a breed bred in the United States and Canada, here is a list of Aussiedoodle resources to help you:

Aussiedoodle Breeders in the USA

- **Doodlesville Aussiedoodles and Goldendoodles**

  http://www.doodlesville.com/

  Located in Southern Virginia

  Doodlesville Aussiedoodles and Goldendoodles pride themselves on producing healthy, well-socialized puppies from health-tested parents.

- **Cottonwood Creek Doodles**

  https://www.cottonwoodcreekdoodles.com/

  Located in Utah

  Cottonwood Creek Doodles specialize in producing healthy companion dogs. The Standard sized Aussiedoodle is the focus of their breeding program.

- **Abounding Grace Doodles**

  http://www.aboundinggracedoodles.com/

  Located in Georgia

  Abounding Grace Doodles produces Aussiedoodle puppies of exceptional temperaments from health-tested parents.

- **Carolina Aussiedoodles of Charleston**

  http://carolinaaussiedoodles.com/

  Located in South Carolina

  Carolina Aussiedoodles of Charleston is a small hobby kennel, breeding only a few litters per year. They are committed to proper health testing practices to ensure healthy puppies.

- **Hope Hill Doodles**

  http://www.hopehilldoodles.com/

  Located in Wisconsin

  Hope Hill Doodles prides themselves on producing companion Aussiedoodles who excel as family pets, therapy dogs, or performance sports animals.

- **Cherry Valley Aussiedoodles**

  http://www.cherryvalleyaussiedoodles.com/about.html

  Located in Ohio

  Cherry Valley Aussiedoodles is a well-rounded breeder. Their main focus is on providing early socialization opportunities to produce confident, healthy puppies.

- **Awesome Doodles**

  https://www.awesomedoodle.com/

  Awesome Doodles place a high priority on producing puppies from health-tested parents of sound temperament.

- **Café au Lait Aussiedoodles**

  https://www.calminiaussiedoodles.com/

  Located in Nevada

  Café au Lait Aussiedoodles proudly produces healthy puppies who make ideal family companions or performance sports dogs. They have been known to produce Aussiedoodles in the rarer Café au Lait color family.

- **Designer Dogs of America**

  https://www.designerdogsofamerica.com/breeders

  Designer Dogs of America is a comprehensive list of Aussiedoodle breeder in the USA.

Aussiedoodle Breeders in Canada

- **Prairie Doodles**

  http://www.prairiedoodles.ca/#prairie-doodles

  Located in Alberta

  Prairie Doodles places a high emphasis on producing well-socialized puppies of excellent health and temperament.

- **Doodleworld**

  http://doodleworld.org/

  Located in Alberta

  Doodleworld is a breeder of several different "Doodle" types. Their Aussiedoodles are backed by a health guarantee.

- **Yankeedoodlepups**

  https://yankeedoodlepup.ca/

  Located in Ontario

  Yankeedoodlepups is a small breeding operation with only a handful of litters per year. Their puppies are from health-tested parents of excellent conformation and temperament.

Aussiedoodle Rescue Shelters in the USA

- **Poo-Mix Rescue**

  https://poomixrescue.com/

  Online resource

  Poo-Mix Rescue is an online resource where people can list Aussiedoodles and other mixes available for adoption. Their main focus is crossbreeds and hybrids.

Aussiedoodle Rescue Shelters in the UK

- **The Doodle Trust**

  https://www.doodletrust.com/

  The only rescue shelter in the UK dealing primarily with crossbreeds, The Doodle Trust places emphasis on finding homes for unwanted Doodles in need of new homes.

Aussiedoodle Registration Services and Breeder Resources in the USA and UK

- **International Designer Canine Registry (IDCR)**

  http://designercanineregistry.com

  The International Designer Canine Registry offers registration services and pedigree tracking for designer dog breeds. They are also a resource for sourcing breeders of Aussiedoodles in your region.

- **National Hybrid Registry (NHR)**

  http://www.nationalhybridregistry.com

  The National Hybrid Registry is a registering body for designer dogs.

- **Designer Dogs—The Kennel Club**

  https://www.thekennelclub.org.uk/our-resources/media-centre/issue-statements/designer-dogs/

  A UK-based registration service, Designer Dogs-The Kennel Club is a registering organization and a resource that seeks to unite dog seekers with dog breeders.

www.ingramcontent.com/pod-product-compliance
Lightning Source LLC
Chambersburg PA
CBHW061046110426
42740CB00049B/2231